Fairhope

A Decade of Stories

Fairhope

A Decade of Stories

Compiled with commentary by Robert M. Glennon.
Contributing writers are acknowledged at the end of their story.

ISBN 978-1945190377

F-12

Published August 2018

www.IntellectPublishing.com

Tribute
to
Donnie Barrett

This book demonstrates ten years of making our Museum of History an educational and enjoyable experience. Volunteers, docents and *Friends of the Museum* have worked diligently under the tutelage of Director Donnie Barrett to help Fairhope tell its story. *The Friends of the Fairhope Museum of History* was chartered in March 2010 as an Alabama 501 (c) 3 not-for-profit organization to support the Museum. It has attracted many talented volunteers, many with advanced degrees, who love history, people and getting involved.

We now celebrate a decade of leadership by Director Donnie Barrett. He has "imagineered" many impressive exhibits and inspired and taught a dynamic group of docents and Friends. He is a natural leader who loves to promote his hometown and encourage others. We are privileged to have such a passionate executive to establish the solid foundation for our Museum as it moves into the future.

Fairhope

The Director of the Museum

Donnie Barrett

History has always been an intrepid topic, which everyone loves, but no one wants to endure the boredom of a speaker, minute details or the antiquity of the story. When the Fairhope City management was seeking a Director for the Museum of History, which was slated to open in April 2008, the question prevailed, "Who do we get to make this interesting? The name of a scholarly, entertaining and dedicated historian, came to mind – Donnie Barrett.

The February 2012 issue of the *Friends Newsletter* carried a feature article about the history of the Old City Hall, built in 1928, which is now, the Museum of History. Finding a Director was no easy task. Actually, it was an easy decision, but acquisition was a bit more difficult. The primary candidate was nearing retirement in his career job, as a graphics artist in Fairhope.

Donnie Barrett has always had a passion for Fairhope! Born in 1949, he attended the Marietta Johnson Organic School and the city public school on Church Street. His afternoons and weekends were spent exploring gullies and clambering through barns and attics to see what he could find. Donnie's grandmother was a Hatchett and was second cousin to Hatchett Chandler, the caretaker of Fort Morgan from WWII until 1953 and author of two books on the fort. "Mr. Chandler inspired me to pursue local history," says Donnie, who would spend hours walking the beach with a pail searching for relics.

He and his parents lived at the Auburn Agricultural Experimental Station where, in addition to absorbing history in that academic setting, he gained affection for area horticulture. He majored in history at Auburn University and the University of South Alabama, with emphasis in Museum Studies. As an artist, he designed the icons and logos for many area historic landmarks. For two decades, his Egyptian art could be seen on walls, signs and sides of buildings in Fairhope.

Donnie spent years producing living history programs at area history sites, forts and battlefields. He served for eight years on the Baldwin County Archeological Preservation Committee and has been on the University of South Alabama's archeological team for thirty years. His main focus was local pottery and historical potters. When the original Fairhope Museum started in the Bell Building at the Organic School in '95, Donnie promptly contributed his creativity to set-up and build all the exhibits.

Archaeological preservation work occupied Donnie's free time during the 80's and 90's. He was involved in several preservation struggles on Dauphin Island and Fort Morgan Peninsula. The original Spanish Fort, many Indian mounds and shell midden systems (shell banks left by Indians) still remain today because of his work.

Donnie was hired for the job of Museum Director in 2007. He says, "I tricked 'em! I now get paid to do what I did all of my life for free!" He and his wife Lottie live near Weeks Bay, where they collect exotic fowl and water plants, and maintain the only tea plantation in Alabama, with over 61,000 tea plants.

Donnie has applied his skill and imagination to the Museum by adding several events and programs unique to our city. The "Mad Professor" at Halloween combines the story of Fairhope with the fun of the holiday. His ability to fill-in, in the unannounced absence of a Tea-for-Two speaker, to expound on any topic, makes him one-of-a-kind! Stand him on a tombstone at the Colony Cemetery and he will talk about the resident like he or she was his personal friend - and he/she very likely was! He has lived Fairhope!

When you visit the Fairhope Museum, this extraordinary Director may greet you at the door with a friendly "Welcome!" or may respond to you from the rafters or from under a display case. He may be encircled by the City Council, or a pack of Cub Scouts. In every way, he makes it interesting!

Bob Glennon, *Published in the Friends of the Fairhope Museum of History Newsletter Vol. 3, Issue 2, April 2012*

Fairhope

Fairhope

A Decade of Stories

Table of Contents

History Stories – Fact and Legend of Fairhope

Fairhope

Fairhope

A Decade of Stories

Fairhope

Chapter 1

Fairhope

If you ever traced the Appalachian Mountains to where they touch the sea, you would find Fairhope, Alabama. It is here that the shoreline dips into Mobile Bay. The hills accent lush green valleys with trees, hedges and flowers that wave in the bay breezes. Azaleas, camellias and annual blooms decorate the town as natural reminders of Southern hospitality.

Fairhope has been a well-kept secret resort since before the War Between the States. Bay-boats - steamboats so called for their shallow draft to allow unimpeded travel in the shallows of the bay, plied the waters bringing visitors from Mobile, twenty miles northwest at the mouth of the Mobile River. Visitors first sought to escape Yellow Fever in the summers through the 1800's, but later came simply to enjoy the fresh air, sandy beaches and social life that permeated the shoreline settlements. Fairhope was one of the last, yet most interesting of those historic stops.

The town of Fairhope was founded in 1894, as a Single Tax Colony with a fair hope of success at being a town of community owned property, beaches, pier and facilities. Twenty-eight settlers, including 8 children were in that first group that came from all over the United States to live in "Utopia", as defined by the Populists who came. The unique mix of residents attracted curiosity seekers, to see what these kooks were doing. Thence came the first tourist gift shop, offering shells, arts, crafts and pottery made of locally mined red, white, blue and grey clays from area creek beds. The hills wept with artesian wells. Fresh water was available without digging. Farms sprang up and businesses were supported by the tourists. Sailing ships procured water before returning to Cuba, the Caribbean and Europe. Timber was a ready-made industry and the waterways granted transportation from as far away as New Orleans, Philadelphia and New York.

The French influence began in 1702 and continued until 1760, when the British took possession of the Gulf Coast east of Louisiana. In 1783, the Spanish, already in Florida seized Mobile and the "no man's land" between Mobile and Florida was sort of forgotten. It became the United States in 1805. Andrew Jackson was sent in 1813 by President Madison, to suppress Indian uprisings, so the land could be settled by Americans. It was then that the Spanish reluctantly moved the sixty miles east to Pensacola.

This cultural mix made for beautiful architecture, interesting dialects and a social lifestyle that combined strong Catholic with Protestant faith practices, cuisine of frontiersmen, Paris and Cajun Louisiana, with Chateauguays and outdoor competitions of the Southern aristocracy. Those traits continue today with the best of each flourishing!

Fairhope was landlocked when it was settled. The only access was by boat; except for a couple of Indian trails that connected Pensacola to Spanish Fort, with the nearest access to those trails being a half-day wagon ride away. The isolation was an asset! The cottages that sprang up in Fairhope were summer places, used from September to Labor Day; then many of those summer residents returned to Mobile, where shipbuilding was active and business on the rivers stimulated the economy. The remote setting of Fairhope attracted free thinkers, liberals by Southern standards, where they could do their own thing. The serenity attracted writers and the views of sunsets, hills and meadows drew sculptors and creative artists. The early 1900's even attracted a nudist camp or two. Most of these interests, talents and skills continue today. When the town was established, the citizens built a pier. With Fate dealing harshly when hurricanes homed-in on the shoreline, the piers were rebuilt each time and today, hundreds of residents comingle with tourists to watch the sun set on weekend evenings. Fairhope Avenue, where shops are open and busy six-days a week, bustle with gift, home decorating and dress shops, stylish sidewalk delis, up-scale restaurants, bakeries, salons and hardware stores. The main street runs west dropping to the bay about a quarter mile from downtown. A beautiful rose garden, fountain and oversize flag always furling in the wind, provide the entrance to the 1483-foot pier protruding into the bay. Youngsters cast nets, fish and feed sea gulls along the side railing, as strolling adults let children scamper to catch a flopping fish or feed a bird looking for a hand-out.

Fairhope cultivates its heritage, but continues with the free-spirit of welcoming outsiders. The original city hall is now the Museum of History and unlike most small towns, the Museum Director sees the museum as an enticing education center as well as the holder of artifacts that make the town's history comes to life. The town's second fire-truck (1935 model) remains in the original "barn" and is still used for parades. Rotating exhibits are featured and draw national acclaim. Special programs highlight events in the town's history, with attendees dressed in period attire and speakers with top-hats pontificating from the podium or balcony. Next door is the town's Welcome Center. The building, now cleaned up a bit, was the town's water works and next to that, the upscale shops and businesses are in the original General Motors auto dealership. It's easy to imagine a spanking new 1939 automobile in the curved glass showroom that now displays home furnishings. The drug store on the corner of Section Street and Fairhope Avenue has been there since

1920. After a recent hurricane, the building siding revealed an original painted advertisement, so instead of replacing the siding, the wall was restored to its original design to the cheers of many residents. On down along the avenue is the "Single Tax District" office. The town today still operates on the Single Tax concept of pro-rating the cumulative tax value of the whole town's real estate. An individual's building improvements are taxed separately.

One of the most interesting and impressive features of Fairhope is the flowers. The town's Utilities Department is run by a horticulturist and has been for many years. The last director is now the mayor in his third term. The downtown area is adorned with hanging baskets of colorful flowers, that are changed with the seasons, before the annual Arts and Crafts Show, before Mardi Gras and near Christmas. The trees downtown, spaced about 20 feet apart are strung with thousands of twinkling lights from late November through the Arts Show in mid-March. In all of Fairhope, harsh penalties are imposed for cutting trees and business must show construction plans that enhance, not remove trees and vegetation.

An annual juried Arts and Crafts Show attracts over 300,000 people to the few streets of downtown Fairhope. The event started in the '60's in store windows, grew onto the sidewalk, and then over-flowed into the streets. Today, about 10 blocks downtown are cordoned off for 3 days for the nationally recognized event.

Art Walks from spring through fall keep shops downtown open on the first Friday of each month from 5 p.m. to 8 p.m. This gives Fairhopians good reason to come out, have some snacks at their favorite shops and support the local businesses. This is a social event that stimulates extra sales and attracts residents to downtown. The local independent book store, Page and Palette is also a great civic supporter. The numerous area writers including nationally known authors, have to schedule well ahead to get their desired signing dates for new publications. The residents who are into the creative arts, provide large enthusiastic audiences for these occasions. The Faulkner State College auditorium, one block over, is often used by speakers, musicians and new book releases.

The creative and eccentric people of Fairhope express themselves in many ways, most drawing encouragement from the community. That includes design of personal homes. Craig Sheldon, sculptor, moved to Fairhope in 1923 and built his house of locally acquired materials, on the edge of a lush green gully. His cottage style homestead is made of limestone, with varying colored shingles giving it an "artsie" motif. When building, if he came upon a bottle or plowshare, that was built right into the wall too. His daughter married, her new husband, also an artist, built a similar cottage next door, with a three-story turret with children's rooms, while the main part of the house has large open rooms of nicely coordinated limestone to accommodate the owner's studio, where he paints twenty-foot fine art in the family room. The windows are out of plumb, which add an attractive whimsical flair to the fun looking residence.

A 1920s resident on the north side of town was Henry Stuart, another eccentric who, according to legend, was told that he was going to die so rather than let his sons watch him fade away; he moved to Fairhope and built a round house about twenty-five feet around and partially underground. He noted that since bees, birds and most animals live in round houses; there must be a good reason. A hurricane came while he was building his strange house and he found refuge in his water well – another confirmation that "round was good"! He hand-sculpted the bricks from local creek-clay, and for years was acclaimed by some old-timers as a hermit. Later, he learned that he was not going to die, so he abandoned his round house and returned to Oregon. This building and legend have been the basis of a gripping story by a local talented writer that has attracted Hollywood movie interests.

In this community that remains close to nature, an environmentally friendly "Green Market" was built five years ago. The open-air building, powered by a contemporary efficient windmill to provide much of the electric needs, is filled with small shops of locally produced paintings, crafts, candies, organic foods and 3 deli restaurants. A surprising number of the shops are staffed with only honor-system boxes that say, "Thank you! Put your payment here." The honor system works in this small friendly community.

Fairhope

City parks are actively shared by all. The Baldwin (County) Pops Orchestra holds free concerts several times each year on the original "Wharf Hill", now called George Park, attracting hundreds with lawn chairs for each performance. There is even a competition for "Best Costume", which causes extravagant portable table setting, chandeliers (tied to tree limbs), and dinner by enthusiasts in formal attire, to be set-up for a "formal evening" at the concert. And the Single Tax philosophy is very visible as there are no houses on the beachfront where the Single Tax Corporation owns the land – it belongs to everyone!

Fairhope experiences a unique fun, thrilling phenomenon in the summertime called a "Jubilee", which rousts out locals in the middle of the night, with no notice except a neighbor's call, "Jubileeee!!!". The event occurs when shrimp, crabs, fish and other sea life from the waters of Mobile Bay are suddenly found scrambling ashore along the coastline. Residents scurry with nets, buckets and gigs to gather up the sea life for an unexpected extraordinary meal. Biologists believe the event occurs when salt water becomes surrounded by fresh water and oxygen becomes depleted. The animals go into an instinctive panic to find oxygenated water; in the process, they beach themselves. The Eastern Shore of Mobile Bay is one of very few places in the world where this event occurs.

The founders of Fairhope sought Utopia. Some say they found it! The only thing for sure, is that we Americans are … in pursuit of happiness. Utopia for most hasn't quite happened yet. But the pursuit continues in this warm, hospitable, beautiful setting, welcoming guests to visit this eclectic little town.

Fairhope's history is not only in print, but is imbedded in the souls of its residents. The city was created on a creative economic and philosophical principles, many of which continue to this day. Residents come because of that imagination. This charisma and these stories, permeate the spirit of our community on Mobile Bay.

Bob Glennon, *Written for the City of Fairhope for Reader's Digest Magazine,* May 27, 2012

Chapter 2

Single Tax Colony

What makes Fairhope different? The first meeting of Fairhope founders was held nine-hundred and ninety-eight miles away! And the first Fairhope *Courier* newspaper was not printed in the South! Yes -- the unique heritage of Fairhope was meticulously planned by a small group of eleven visionaries who had to pack and travel almost a thousand miles before they were "home."

The community of Fairhope was conceived by a group in Des Moines, Iowa, who used the theories of economist and social reformer, Henry George and his book, *Progress and Poverty.* George believed that land speculation was the source of most economic woes, and that the solution was that no taxes should be levied other than a "single tax" on land. According to legend, after months of work on the governing document for their new colony, it got its name when one of the original Des Moines group proclaimed that he thought it had a "fair hope" of success. And so the Fairhope Industrial Corporation was born.

Led by newspaperman Ernest B. Gaston, (who started publishing The Fairhope *Courier* before he ever left Iowa), the visionaries looked for land throughout the South and Midwest before settling on a high bluff overlooking Mobile Bay. And in November 1894, twenty-eight people from around the country met at Battle's Wharf and began to build their own Utopia. Those first colonists were soon referred to as "Single Taxers," and they immediately attracted supporters and financial backers from around the country, drawing an eclectic assemblage of industrious, creative, and free-thinking people to Fairhope.

The Fairhope founders were not able to create a true single tax community as defined by Henry George, but they attempted to come as close as they could. The acquired land in the name of the Fairhope Single Tax Corporation (it was officially called the Fairhope Industrial Association until 1904), then leased the land to those who wanted to use or live on the land. Lessees have a 99-year renewable lease on the land, but have ownership only of improvements.

Fairhope became a resort community almost from the start. The founders quickly realized that the key to their survival depended upon a connection to the outside world. One of their first undertakings was the construction of the first Fairhope wharf, which allowed visitors to come by Bay boat from Mobile to relax in the small Bay cottages and hotels that sprung up along the bluff top. Vacationers came to Fairhope in the early days for many of the same reasons they do today: its pleasant climate, peaceful surroundings, and impressive scenery. Artists, writers, and craftsmen found Fairhope to be an inspiring haven for their work. Even a few nudists found it attractive!

The City of Fairhope was established with around 500 residents in 1908, taking over responsibility for all municipal services. In the 1930's, the City became the caretaker of Fairhope's greatest assets: the beachfront park, the parklands on the bluff above the beach, Henry George Park, Knoll Park, and the quarter-mile-long pier--
all gifts of the Single Tax Colony, which continues to have an active presence in the City.

Today, the Single Tax Corporation owns about 4500 acres of land in and around Fairhope. This includes the downtown area and a little less than half of the remainder of the City. The rent paid to the Single Tax Corporation by lessees includes an amount due for state, county and local taxes, an administration fee to operate the Corporation office, and a "demonstration fee," intended to demonstrate the usefulness of the single tax concept. Funds from the demonstration fee are used to enhance the community by supporting things such as the public parks, the public library, Thomas Hospital, and *our* historical Museum.

Bob Glennon, *Portions of the contents of this article were taken from the City of Fairhope and the Fairhope Single Tax Corporation websites. Published in the Friends of the Fairhope Museum of History Newsletter Vol. 3, Issue 3, June 2012.*

Chapter 3

Fairhope's Devotion to Henry George

Everyone who visits or lives in Fairhope has heard about the "Single Tax Colony" based on the principles of the political economist, Henry George. They will likely also see Henry George Park on the bluff and the white marble obelisk in the corner of the park. On the side are chiseled quotes of Henry George about Land, Labor and Capital. The curious would then wonder why Fairhope would have a monument to a 19th century political economist.

Henry George is little known, except for a few enclaves like Fairhope and a few academic circles. But in the 1890s, he was very well known. His first book, "Progress and Poverty" was one of the most widely read books in the country. It was published in 1879 and within a few years, there were thousands of study groups discussing how to form a better social structure and eliminate poverty. One such group led by E. B. Gaston of Des Moines, Iowa and several of the members of that group later became the founders of Fairhope. They focused on George's land policy. He believed that land was the source of all wealth and was the only thing that should be taxed by the government. This theory of taxing land only, became known by the late 1880s as "Single Tax "and became a significant factor in U.S. politics with over 500,000 people claiming to be Single Taxers.

Gaston and his fellow reformers in Des Moines were focused on creating a communal Utopian society and decided to include the Henry George proposed Single Tax as one of the founding principles of Fairhope. They had already decided to have a corporation, which became the Fairhope Industrial Association, to own all of the city land and lease it to residents for a yearly amount based on the land value. This was a modified version of the single tax. They were hoping that Henry George would endorse Fairhope as a good demonstration of the Single Tax, but he didn't. Mr. George wanted implementation at the national level and didn't endorse any small experiments with the "Single Tax", fearing that it would discredit his ideology.

Henry George lived the last 17 years of his life in New York City where he wrote other books explaining his theories and was heavily involved in local and national politics. He died in 1897, during his second run for mayor of New York City. After his death, the single tax movement went into a slow decline. Fairhope also struggled with the Single Tax experiment. The Fairhope Industrial Association could not get control of all the land around the city and decided to form a conventional city government in 1908. The Fairhope Industrial Association changed its name to the Fairhope Single Tax Colony (FSTC) in 1904 which retained their allegiance to the movement. Basing property taxes on land values alone, became unlawful in Alabama. So the lease amounts charged to the lessees became the county and local tax assessment amounts, plus other fees. The small additional fee that is currently charged by the FSTC is for the stated purpose of demonstrating Henry George's principles.

Even with the many setbacks, leaders of Fairhope and the FSTC through the years, continue their devotion to Henry George and his philosophy. E. B. Gaston continued to write newspaper editorials stating that Fairhope was doing well as a Single Tax colony. Other newspapers and magazines published stories about Fairhope's success with a modified single tax system. People from Fairhope often attended Henry George Conferences where they spoke about how well Fairhope was doing based on implementation of Henry George's principles. Sam Dyson, a long time Fairhope lawyer, a believer in Henry George's economic principles and one-time head of the FSTC, is believed to be the sponsor of permanent monument to Henry George.

In 1982, the FSTC commissioned a monument in the park to honor Henry George. The Obelisk was selected and designed by a committee and was dedicated on Sept 2nd, 1989, the 150th anniversary of his birth. There was a full day of celebrations with speeches, music, dancing and a birthday cake that was cut by Craig Shelton. The Governor of Alabama declared that day to be Henry George day in the State of Alabama. It was a great celebration of Fairhope's unending devotion to the social and economic principles of Henry George.

Curt Cochran, *Published in Friends of the Fairhope Museum of History Newsletter Vol.5, Issue 4, August 2014*

Chapter 4

Fairhope Single Tax Colony Cemetery

The body floating face down in the Bay on July 4, 1895 was that of John Hunnell. The new town now had an emergency item on its agenda – a funeral!

Fairhope's founders, including Mr. Hunnell, had arrived on the bluff overlooking what would become the Fairhope Pier, in November 1894. But, just eight months later, on Independence Day 1895, the Single Tax Colonists found themselves delaying their planned 4th of July celebration at the beach to select a site to bury their friend. They had already chosen one of the most beautiful spots in Fairhope as the community cemetery. Their dilemma now was that lumber for making a casket on short notice was not available. So in keeping with the spirit of the holiday, one of the wooden picnic tables from down on the beach was cut up and made into a coffin. He had gone down to the Bay for a bath; other than that, no one ever knew exactly what happened. John was laid to rest that same afternoon.

The burial site at the corner of today's Oak and Section Streets was the first grave on approximately four acres that were set aside for use as the cemetery. The property was on the north edge of town, as the terrain dictated the town limits in that direction. Section Street was the main, dirt road north through downtown and curved northwest through the cemetery dead-ending at the gully.

The first graves were located on the east side of the road and houses were originally slated for the west side of that dirt street. If homes were ever built there, is unknown. Director Donnie Barrett says archeological digs at the spot reveal evidence of house-wares and construction materials, but there are no records of residences on that part of the street before that too was taken for grave sites.

Fourteen of the original twenty-eight Fairhope founders are buried in the Colony Cemetery. Therein also lies the remains of Marietta Johnson, creator of the internationally renowned Organic School, Marie Howland, founder of the town library, Craig Sheldon, sculpture and artist, as well as ex-mayors, doctors and some contemporary residents of the Fairhope Single Tax Corporation (FSTC). Mr. Hunnell's body was later relocated by his family, but because of his legacy as a founder, his gravestone remains. It is noteworthy that E.B. Gaston's son, Cornelius, who came to the Colony at the age of 10 and continued his dad's work with the FSTC until his death, is buried *not here*, but in Memorial Gardens on Greeno Road.

The cemetery has the ornate walk-in entrance gate on Section Street and a drive-entrance on Church Street. The property will accommodate approximately 2500 gravesites. The requisites have the unique provision that vaults or caskets must be at least fourteen inches below the surface and a spouse is buried on top of his/her predeceased partner, to save space. A member or lessee of the FSTC can still be buried there provided he/she meets the eligibility guidelines of the FSTC Cemetery Committee. The care and maintenance of individual graves and monuments are the responsibility of family and friends. The general care and maintenance of the cemetery is partly funded with donations to the FSTC for that purpose.

Bob Glennon, *Published in the Friends of the Fairhope Museum of History Newsletter, Vol. 4, Issue 1, February 2014*

Chapter 5

The Fairhope "People's Railroad"
1912 – 1923

In August 1912, a petition was signed by almost 100 people to establish a "People's Railroad" in Fairhope. By 1914, it was well underway. The rails began at the far end of the wharf and ran up the hill on Fairhope Avenue to Bancroft Street, south to Morphy Avenue, then east, but never got further than School Street, barely turning onto Morphy.

The actual service car No.1 used by the People's Railroad, here loaded with bags and barrels, is now on display in our Museum

Morphy Avenue was the main road into town from the East. The original plan was for the railroad to continue east when funds became available, to "Bellforest Road" (Highway 181), north to AL highway 104, then east to Silverhill and Robertsdale, where it would connect to another railroad.

Fairhope

The first railcar to run on the railroad, People's Railroad Car No. 1, was built by Frank Brown in his sawmill near the southeast corner of Morphy and Greeno Roads. It was built on the chassis of a Thomas-Flyer automobile.

According to the *Fairhope Courier*, the rails for the project were scheduled to arrive in Mobile around August 7, 1914 on the steamer, "Mallory" and promptly be loaded onto a barge destined to Fairhope. In fact, the steamboat, "Nemesis", arrived at Fairhope on August 14, with the barge and the first mile of rails. The *Courier* reported that on September 4, "track laying was suspended… until the service car was available to bring forward the rails from the wharf, as pushing them up the grade on a hand car was proving too slow and expensive a job especially as the distance increased." A trestle was built from a short distance out on the wharf to the top of the hill, to engineer the required grade incline. The tracks were narrow gauge spacing, with 80 pound weight rails. On Saturday, September 18, the *Courier* said, "Last Saturday, the People's Railroad Car Number 1 was hastily outfitted with rough temporary seats and an older car added as a trailer with seats, met the 'Apollo' and brought up a full load of passengers. And it has since met the boat regularly, morning and evening, handling passengers, freight and supplies for the railroad construction crew." The fare from the pier, up the steep grade to the water tank in the center of town, was 5 cents.

The full mile of track was finished on October 9, stopping on Morphy, near School Street. This completed the initial project funds. The pressures of the Great War in Europe side-tracked additional funding while national attention was turned to matters "over there."

After the Doughboys returned home, attempts were made to stimulate further financing for the Railroad, but keen competition from other wharves, truck lines and use of personal automobiles, diluted interest. The railroad went out of business in 1923.

Bob Glennon, *Published in the Friends of the Fairhope Museum of History Newsletter Vol. 3, Issue 4, August 2012*

Chapter 6

Marietta Johnson's Organic School of Education

Have you thought about Fairhope as being an *EPCOT*, almost seventy years earlier than Walt Disney envisioned his city of tomorrow? The Fairhope founders also saw an **E**xperimental **P**rototype **C**ommunity **O**f **T**omorrow that would never be complete but would continue to grow as ideas and inventions were put into practice. This gets us to one of the most progressive and surviving concepts in our city of tomorrow – the Marietta Johnson Organic School of Education.

Marietta Louise Pierce Johnson was born in 1864 in St. Paul Minnesota. Her early education was in public schools in Minnesota and even as a young girl, she dreamed of becoming a teacher herself. Upon her graduation from the State Normal School in 1885, now St. Cloud State College, she did become a teacher. Between 1890 and 1899, she observed students in practice teaching and on occasion would take over a class to demonstrate her ideas; she was an inspiring and creative teacher, full of new ideas on schooling. In 1903, she and her husband spent the winter in Fairhope, a new town founded on the single-tax theory. The progressives in town invited her to open an experimental school to explore some of her educational ideas. She accepted and in 1907 moved permanently to Fairhope where she became the director of the school. She had six students the first day at her "Organic School" and after a few years, enrolled as many as 200 students per year. With community support and her tireless fundraising, the school was always tuition free to its students, yet received no public funds. It was called "organic" in that the central aim was to "minister to the health of the body, develop the finest mental grasp and preserve the sincerity and un-self-consciousness of the emotional life." She believed grades, report cards and promotions created the tension of self-consciousness, so they were omitted. Students were judged only for their individual abilities, and emphasis was placed on the satisfactions of learning and growth. The school incorporated in 1909.

Ms. Johnson's vision of a new education, based on her organic school experiment, took on national prominence with the publication in 1915 of the *Deweys' Schools of Tomorrow*. John Dewey and his daughter Evelyn after visiting and studying the school wrote extensively and positively about the experiment. Ms. Johnson established a second Organic School, following the Fairhope model, in Greenwich, CT. By the late 1920's, she was dividing her time between Alabama and Connecticut. She became internationally renowned for progressive education. The Organic School in Fairhope progressed well at its location between School and Bancroft Streets until Ms. Johnson's death in 1938. Then her fundraising skills became more apparent. Enrollment dropped below 100, cash flow trickled and faculty morale fell.

As with any great undertaking, there have been bumps along the road. Without Marietta there to continually inspire students and large donors, enrollment, leadership and funding have become reoccurring concerns. In the 1940's, a Board and 3-person Executive Committee managed the school. For a time, the Organic School property was used as security to obtain a loan from the Single Tax Corporation to pay off debts and sponsor operation of the school. In the 1950's many of Fairhope's prosperous families rallied around the school and enrollment rebounded to 120 students. But with that effort the Corporation yielded to pressure and violated one of Mrs. Johnson's basic tenets; teachers were instructed to grade students and issue report cards to parents. The format switched back and forth in the early '60's between the classes and hand-on-training practices that Ms. Johnson had insisted upon. Enrollment ranged between 110 and 140 students.

Over the years, the Organic School continued to receive help from generous benefactors. A major bequest from the estate of longtime supporter Georgianna Ives funded a capital improvement program. The Board was able to reclaim the school's assets from the Single Tax Corporation in 1967. In the late 1970's, Harold Dahlgren donated funds to retool the workshop, restore the old high school building and help the school become solvent again. In 1989, the Board accepted the City  of Fairhope's offer of $334,000 to rebuild the school at a new site on Pecan Street, so that Faulkner State Community College could open a branch campus downtown on the original 10-acre Organic School site. The Ives Probate Trust Fund continues to underwrite about half of the School's budget and to offer generous scholarships to worthy students each year.

The school got negative publicity in 2004 when it used treated wood in the organic wood shop, where students were exposed to dust and treatment chemicals. This was a major contributing factor to a drop in enrollment, teachers quitting and the PTA Roundtable being dissolved. High school level classes were eliminated thereafter due to lack of funding and students. "Home School" high school was conducted for a few years, but was discontinued at the end of the 2011 – 2012 school year. Classes from Kindergarten through 9th grade are now taught at the school.

Our Museum Director Donnie Barrett was a teacher at the Organic School during the years 2003 through 2006. He says, "Teachers were required to send home report cards, but that lasted only for a short while. 'Progress Reports', not report cards, now go home to parents."

The Organic School continues as a haven for creative thinking and free-spirited activities. And the School, along with the Single Tax Corporation, are the most prominent remaining vestiges of our EPCOT in Alabama!

* *Portions of the text in the "Organic School" article were taken from" the Harbinger, Part II", by Dr. Joseph Newman, professor and chair of the Department of Educational Leadership and Foundation, University of South Alabama, October 28, 1997.*

Bob Glennon, *Published in the Friends of the Fairhope Museum of History Newsletter Vol. 4, Issue 2, April 2013*

Chapter 7

Literary Treasures in the Fairhope Museum

The Fairhope Museum of History has acquired another treasure! The Fairhope Public Library has generously given over to our care, the remaining 479 original books and bound magazines of one of the first public libraries in Alabama, established in Fairhope in 1900.

In many ways, their journey to their final home is as fascinating, adventurous, and full of hope and ideals as the books themselves and the woman who brought them to Fairhope - Marie Howland.

When Marie Stevens Case married Edward Howland in 1865, he was a professional book buyer in New York City and had a personal library of thousands of books he had collected in America as well as on book-buying  trips to Amsterdam, Leipzig, Paris, Oxford and London. The couple lived for many years in New York and New Jersey, always surrounding them-selves with other intellectuals and reformers of the time.

Edward did not live to see Fairhope, but in 1888 he and Marie moved (with their library) to help establish a Utopian community in Topolobampo, Mexico. Edward died just two years later; Marie stayed in Mexico for three more years, editing their newspaper and setting up a library there with the Howland books as its nucleus.

Disillusioned with what she saw as the failure of that community to live up to its ideals, she literally took her books and went home— putting the books in storage and travelling around visiting friends who shared her progressive beliefs in women's rights and social equality. It was one of these friends who told her in 1898 about a newspaper he subscribed to: *The Fairhope Courier.* Marie wrote to its editor, E.B. Gaston.

Then aged 63, widowed but newly inspired, Marie made the final and most rewarding move of her life. She arrived in Fairhope in 1899, built a small house with plenty of bookshelves on the corner of Summit and Magnolia, and sent for the books (weighing over 1100 lbs) she had kept in storage in Kansas. Some were damaged, but in her words, "I have put new stitches in the rheumatic back of Julius Caesar; pasted the ragged clothing on the body of Juvenal, and straightened out the folds and wrinkles in the face of many an old favorite."

The community was so grateful to Marie for her donation and her efforts that many citizens stepped forward to volunteer their help and their money. With added funds from the Single Tax Corporation, in 1900 it truly became a public library.

Others made generous donations of books and materials, and our library soon outgrew Marie's home, then another separate structure built on that property, and then the City Hall location on Section Street. When our library moved to its wonderful new home on the corner of Fairhope Avenue and Bancroft in 2007, Marie's beloved books again moved with it. And now those precious books--fragile, long forgotten by most-- have found an honored home at the Fairhope Museum of History.

We like to think Marie would be pleased to know that the books she loved so much, protected, and shared, are back among the stories and artifacts of her friends and fellow Fairhope pioneers.

A Decade of Stories

Docent Mary Ann Maradik, who has taken on the daunting task of organizing and cataloguing the Howland collection, adds, "We are relishing these treasures as we catalogue the books for our archives and ready them to be exhibited in the Museum.

Most of the books were published in the 1800's and many before this time. Given their age, these books are very fragile and are wonderful evidence of the value and wisdom of our human history.

The topics of these scholarly individual books and volume sets include history, geography, political science, health, travel, phrenology, religion, prayer books, science, novels, literary works, theatre, poetry, encyclopedias, dictionaries and much more. Since the Howlands traveled extensively, there are many books written in German, French, Old English and Greek, in addition to American English. We even have Marie's handwritten card catalogue, using the organizational system she devised.

We are so grateful to Marie and to the Library, and we look forward to sharing this wonderful collection with visitors to the Fairhope Museum of History."

Susan Pearce, *Published in the Friends of the Fairhope Museum of History Newsletter Vol. 2, Issue 1, February 2011*

Chapter 8

The Bay Boat Era

The colorful history of Fairhope is enriched by bay boats like the
Fairhope, pictured above, launched in June 1901.

Photograph: Courtesy MobileBayVintagePhotos.com

At the time Fairhope was founded in November 1894, several boats
served the Eastern Shore. Daphne, Montrose, Battles Wharf, Point
Clear and Zundel's Landing, all had bay boat service to and from
Mobile. These towns were served over time by *The Ocean Wave,
Annie, Heroine, Apollo, Bay Queen, Pleasure Bay, James A Carney*
and others. But the Single-Taxers wanted daily reliable service to and
from Mobile. They didn't feel they could rely on private bay boats to

meet their wishes or needs. Also, some of the Fairhopeans wanted to reduce the winter rate increases and "a competing boat would do that," they said.

On October 8, 1900, those locals interested in building a public steamer gathered. Since the Fairhope Industrial Association constitution forbade interest-bearing debt, a trustee plan was adopted, which would offer investors a reasonable profit. However, all earnings from the boat after operating expenses, were pledged to retire the stock. The boat would then be turned over to the Association.

The 95-ton bay boat "Fairhope" was launched on June 27, 1901, but it was not without trauma nor was it as successful as they had hoped. On December 12, 1901, the *Heroin* and *Fairhope*, proceeding on their regular trips across the bay, had a near miss. "The *Fairhope* left the dock a few minutes ahead of the *Heroine*. A short time later when *Heroine* was approaching *Fairhope* to pass, she blew for her side," reported the *Baldwin Times*. "*Fairhope* answered and gave the right of way. Just as *Heroine* was about halfway past, the *Fairhope* pulled in, ostensibly to get the suction from *Heroine* and in doing so, struck *Heroine* a little back of the wheelhouse. The only damage was a couple of planks broken on *Heroine*, but *Fairhope* careened so badly that the passengers on *Heroine* who saw the accident thought she would surely turn over." Notwithstanding this event, the boat continued daily service between Fairhope and Mobile.

In 1905, the *Fairhope* received a complete overhaul of the boiler and machinery. This overhaul cost $6,000, which had not been insured because the trustees thought insurance was too expensive. Shortly after it returned to service, the *Fairhope* burned to the waterline on November 21, 1905 while moored at the Fairhope pier. But the Colony itself did not suffer in the deal. Settlements were made out of court and the trustees were relieved of further responsibilities.

In 1906, another bay boat was purchased on behalf of the Single-Taxers by the Fairhope Improvement Company, which had no legal connection with the Fairhope Industrial Association (later called the Fairhope Single Tax Corporation). The "*Fairhope II*," an iron hull craft, ran directly between Fairhope and Mobile, leaving Fairhope early each morning, except Sunday, and returned leaving Mobile in mid-afternoon. This allowed for passenger connections to the train heading north out of Mobile on weekday mornings. The boat also left Fairhope for Mobile on Saturday afternoon late and returned on Sunday morning, allowing for an overnight stay in the city. The adult fare was twenty-five cents each way and children between five and twelve years old paid fifteen cents. The boat served well until mechanical problems demanded that it be retired in 1910. It was returned to creditors in Mobile where it made a brief, but unsuccessful attempt to resume service to the Eastern Shore. Other bay boats continued to serve Fairhope daily, even after the Cochran Bridge Causeway was opened in 1927. Unfortunately, business dropped off rapidly as personal automobiles and commercial trucks had easy access over the bay.

The last of the steam-powered bay boats, *"Eastern Shore"* sailed her final trip across the bay on Thursday, October 12, 1933. A romantic and historic era ended as the sun set on shallow draft steamers on Mobile Bay.

In April 2015, the Fairhope Museum of History launched its own maritime exhibit about *The Bay Boat Era.* Six precise model bay boats, memorabilia and relics were displayed to remind us of the good ole days on the bay, with chautauquas and local culture built around the boats.

Models are built to scale, based on original specifications. The *Fairhope I and Fairhope II* represent the entrepreneurship of the Single Tax Colony to bring passengers and money to the businesses on Fairhope Avenue. The *Pleasure Bay, Heroine, Baldwin, Apollo* and the *General Lee* will also be on display with placards of their stories in the development of Fairhope.

Specially designed shallow-draft paddle-wheel steamboats were used for passenger traffic from Mobile and New Orleans to the Eastern Shore even before the founding of Fairhope.

Mobilians came in the summers to avoid the Yellow Fever that was believed to be brought by visiting ships from Europe and the Caribbean. The vegetation and higher elevation of the Eastern Shore greatly reduced the infestation of mosquitoes that in fact, were the causes of the diseases in the city.

The bay-boats provided transportation and entertainment, as families would gather at the wharfs to meet fathers returning from Mobile and distant relatives who took the train to Mobile, then the bay-boats.

The earliest steamboats to ply the rivers from Mobile were the *Alabama (1818), Harriott* and *Cotton Plant, (1821).* Fairhope bay boat historian Peco Forsman says the *Ocean Wave, Annie, Heroine, James A. Carney, Fairhope I* and *Fairhope II* had a positive impact on the economy of Baldwin County before and after the settlement of Fairhope in 1894.

The exhibit featured specific bay-boats that served Fairhope during the era, providing a life-line to the local economy via export of pottery made from nearby clays and the import of curiosity seekers, Mobilians coming to summer cottages and tourists to stare at Single-Taxers, who settled into their view of "Utopia."

The opening of the Cochran Bridge Causeway for automobile traffic between Mobile and the Eastern Shore in 1928 preempted the need for boat transit of people and freight. Until then, the golden age of paddlewheel steamboats prevailed on Mobile Bay. ~

Bob Glennon, *A series of articles appeared in the Friends Newsletter in 2015 regarding the Bay Boat Feature Exhibit on display from Mid-2015 to Mid-2016 in the Museum of History. This article was published in three Issues of the Newsletter and are edited here to consolidate content. These were printed in the February – March, April – May and June – July 2015 Issues of the Friends Newsletter.*

Chapter 9

The Fairhope Pier

When E.B. Gaston and his followers arrived on the Eastern Shore in 1894, they quickly realized that because of the sandy soil and many gullies that were here, they would have to turn away from farming to make the Colony work. The Fairhope Industrial Association decided to build a pier where boats could transport people from Mobile to Fairhope and they charged them a docking fee to use the pier. In 1895, they built the first of what would to be nine piers to date; the first 5 were used extensively for bringing people and goods to the

A Decade of Stories

Eastern Shore since the only way to get here was by water until the causeway was completed in 1927.

The first pier lasted until 1906, when it was destroyed by a hurricane. It was immediately rebuilt but was destroyed by fire in 1910 along with the steamer, *General Lee*. The first ice cream plant in the State was located at the foot of that pier in 1907. When rebuilding in 1910, there was a dance hall, bath house and bowling lane housed in a building called "The Casino", constructed on shore near the new pier.

In 1914, the "People's Railroad" was built, which ran from the end of the pier to what is now Bancroft Avenue. This pier was in use until the 1916 hurricane washed it away. Subsequently, piers were destroyed in 1926 and 1936, also by hurricanes. The 1936 pier, the last of the wooden piers, survived over 30 years and was replaced in 1968 with our first of three concrete piers. At this time, a bulkhead was built out in the water and filled in with dirt. That is where the parking lot, fountain and rose garden now stand. Also at that time, the "Casino" was removed.

In 2004, Hurricane Ivan severely damaged the pier, and it took nearly a year to complete repairs. After it reopened in 2005, Hurricane Katrina again destroyed it. It was immediately rebuilt, and that pier is the one that stands today, used by our citizens for fishing, strolling and viewing one of the most sensational sunsets in our country.

Louie Blaze, *Published in the Friends of the Fairhope Museum of History Newsletter Vol. 4, Issue 1, February 2013*

Chapter 10

Populism or Henry George?

It is often said that Fairhope was founded by people from Iowa who came here to prove the soundness of the Henry George philosophy and that Fairhope was based on Henry George principles. A review of our history may show that there is more to the story.

During the 1870's, a large political movement took place as a response to rampant growth in the corporate, banking and railroad industries. The Farmers Alliance organizations in most every state started the People's Party known as Populism. Their presidential candidate in 1892 was General James B. Weaver, owner of the *Farmer's Tribune* newspaper, who hired a young Ernest Berry Gaston to run the newspaper while Weaver was on the campaign trail. Gaston was already the Secretary of the Iowa Populist Committee and a member of the local "Investigation Club," looking

Director Donnie Barrett speaking on Populism at the Fairhope Public Library, as a part of the 2015 Lecture Series on Fairhope History, March 3, 2015.

at communal experiments, philosophies, and better ways to organize government. He was quite familiar with Henry George's 1879 "Progress & Poverty," one of the most popular books in print.

When Weaver lost the election to Grover Cleveland, Gaston heard his calling and struck out to improve society and "put good principals to work." After looking at 175 communal failures and many philosophic options, Gaston designed and sold stock in "The American

Cooperative Company." This was not a single tax structured venture, but a purely "Bellamy-style" socialist colony. Gaston promoted it hard during 1893, but after a year, it too never got off paper and failed.

In late 1893, Gaston wrote his paper "True Cooperative Individualism," which even today is a masterpiece document which does not mention Henry George or Single Tax. He was weighing out the balance of socialism and capitalism. He thought Henry George was a bit too individualistic but still liked the land value biased taxation, that was called the "single tax" by Henry George admirers. At this point Gaston wrote the "Fairhope Plan" of applying the single tax, which "wasn't George" to many of Gaston's distracters. Gaston founded the Fairhope Industrial Association with ten of his Populist friends, who was interested in "cooperation" on January 4, 1894. When they got to the Eastern Shore, they installed Populist platitudes; money system, People's Railroad, Bayboats, Home Phone System and several cooperatives, which were not single tax attributes.

Henry George never came to or acknowledged the Fairhope Colony so it is a misplaced honor to credit him with Fairhope's high level of success. Henry George was highly influential to many, one of the most famous people of the 19th century, but founded no social experiments or colonies to prove his theories would work. Ernest Berry Gaston did. He was "boots on the ground" demonstrating good principles put into practice and good theories at work. Maybe we may not need to call Fairhope a Henry George experiment, but give credit where due, to Ernest Gaston who founded the Utopian dream of Fairhope, and whose principles still stand firm today.

Donnie Barrett, *Published in the Friends of the Fairhope Museum of History Newsletter Vol. 6, Issue 2, April – May 2015*

Chapter 11

Old City Hall

To begin a treatise of Fairhope history, we must start with the current roof over our heads. This has been the location for many a debate and outright arguments by our colorful residents for the past eighty-four years!

The Old City Hall, with its unique Spanish Mission stucco façade, has attracted the question, "What's that?", since its construction in 1928. It was built as the first Fairhope Municipal Building to consolidate the City government: the Mayor's office, the City Council Chamber, the Fire Department and Police headquarters. The Fairhope Single Tax Colony donated the land and the initial structure was a "grievous" expenditure of $4,279.

Two cells were built on the first floor behind the Mayor's office for use in the unlikely event there was ever a need. And before long, they *did* accommodate a few well-meaning inebriated citizens until they were able to find their way home the next morning. It wasn't easy to be thrown in the Fairhope jail. The liberal founding spirit was rather tolerant of most misdemeanors, with the police chief merely giving the offender a ride home and a verbal reprimand for his actions.

The first Mayor to serve in the new building was M.F. Northrup. The last Mayor to preside over the City Council in the building was Richard Macon. When Mayor James Nix took office in 1972, the City had already moved City Hall into the old First National Bank of Fairhope building, at the current Colonial Bank location on Fairhope Avenue. In 1992, the fire department moved to its present Ingleside Avenue site. The police stayed in the old building until 2002.

After that, the building became a storage dump for unused city property while a more permanent use was debated. Citizens and city council members postulated using the building as an art center or a private gallery. One gentleman offered $100,000 to turn it into a Fairhope Writer's Cottage. As with many issues in Fairhope, there was no shortage of strongly held opinions, which resulted in many raucous fights at Council meetings. Raucous fights at City Council meetings have always been a beloved Fairhope tradition.

In the meantime, the Fairhope Museum, founded in 1991, was housed in the Bell building on the old Organic School campus. Eventually, the City allocated $700,000 to be used to renovate the aging structure and restore its Spanish stucco façade. That amount was quickly matched by another $700,000 donation from the Single Tax Corporation, to add a two-story addition facing onto Bancroft Street, which would effectively double usable display space to accommodate the Museum's ever-growing collections. "Museum Plaza," a park created to visually connect the Museum with the new Fairhope library, was then planned for the site as well.

Donnie Barrett, lifelong Fairhope resident, professional Historian, Museum Curator, and acknowledged expert on All Things Fairhope, was recruited as Director, to oversee the creation of the Museum and its subsequent operation. The Museum, now an official part of the City of Fairhope, opened in the building in April, 2008.

Take a minute to stare at the Section Street façade and imagine the personalities who entered these doors. Ms. Winifred Duncan, when not canoeing on the Bay in the nude, would appear fully dressed to conduct City business; Marmaduke Dyson and Oswald Forster, known for getting into fist-a-cuffs on the streets of town, usually remained civil when they came to see the Mayor, and Billy Stimpson would drop by to complain that the boards were again falling out of the nudist camp fence on Morphy.

It's easy to understand how this Grand Old Lady of Fairhope—after 80 years and numerous incarnations, has now become the epicenter for reliving our City's history!

Bob Glennon, *Published in the Friends of the Fairhope Museum of History Newsletter Vol. 3, Issue 1, February 2012*

Chapter 12

Fairhope Pottery

Pottery shards are everywhere! – in the gullies, backyards, creek beds and even in the Bay. Fairhope's roots are in its clay, and residents since the Single-Taxers came in 1894, have been able to literally mold their destinies with the clays of the Eastern Shore. Our Fairhope Museum of History has inaugurated a new Pottery Exhibit that will remain open until next March, to tell the story of area pottery and its importance to the Eastern Shore.

Museum Director Donnie Barrett points to the famous logo of Alabama City on the locally made historic jug

The centerpiece of the exhibit is an expansion of the "Alabama City" permanent exhibit in the Museum. Alabama City was a failed real estate development in1840 on the land that later became Fairhope.

The French potter Augustine Mareschal took advantage of what he hoped would be name recognition and inscribed the stamp of "Alabama City" or "BAMA City" on his pottery. The premier collectible piece with this stamp is owned by the Birmingham Art Museum and is valued at $33,000. His pottery kilns on Fly Creek, the current location of the Fairhope Yacht Club, were the only shop or mill in the immediate area at that time. Mareschal's pottery production initiated a great expansion of that business on the Eastern Shore. Pottery production peaked in 1888 when one third of the population of Baldwin County was employed in the pottery industry.

This major industry was possible by abundant natural resources. There is a major vein of clay about 10 feet thick stretching from Clay City on the Fish River to Daphne, along with salt, fire-wood and water access, which was needed for transporting the heavy pottery to market.

The first clay pots baked on the Easter Shore were made in the 1200s by the Mississippian Indians. Their pots were very utilitarian and were used for storing food and water. They were decorated with little figures on the top of the bowls called effigy heads. These two to three inches tall effigy heads have been found washed up on the beach at Point Clear. About 50 of these figures are on display in our Museum pottery exhibit.

The French explored Mobile Bay in the 1600s and established the first pottery and brick making facility on Fly Creek. Fly Creek is the nominal English translation of the French "Volante Bayou" (the name for the area) with the French "volante" translated as "flying". Volanta Avenue in north Fairhope today, goes down to the Fairhope Yacht Club, where the French first located their kilns. The first pottery made in the Americas by non-natives was made by the French on Fly Creek in 1717. The French also made bricks for Fort Conde in 1717 and referred to their location as "Ecor Rouge" (Red Bluffs) which is now Montrose.

The pottery made in the 1700s and early 1800s with a lead glaze was termed earthenware. The innovative potter Augustine Mareschal developed the technique to use salt glaze and produce stoneware.

38

Besides the salt glaze, the enabling technology was the "Ground Hog Kiln" which could bake pots with temperatures up to 2300 degrees. He built the first stoneware kilns on Fly Creek in the 1830s. By 1850 Mareschal had moved on the Montrose to join two other French potters: Augustine La Coste and Lewis LeFevre. The Scottish potter, Peter McAdams joined them when he immigrated to Montrose in the 1860s. These men and several other pioneers made Montrose a major center for pottery which expanded dramatically in the late 1800s. The demand for practical pottery decreased in the early 1900s and the last pottery kiln in Montrose closed in 1920 with Prohibition killing the demand for whiskey jugs.

Pottery returned to Fairhope in the early 1900s with Frank Brown and his brick making operation. His brick making machine (Circa 1886) is on display at the Museum. Making pottery pieces as an art form also returned with Edith Harwell who taught pottery at the School of Organic Education and continued to make pots after she left teaching. One of her students was Tom Jones, who was a potter in Fairhope until he moved to Clay City. John Reznor is another Fairhope potter who has works on display in the exhibit.

Pot making also came to Clay City, which is located off highway 33 near the mouth of the Fish River. Joseph Gabel made pots there in 1882. Perhaps better known are the couple, Jim and Catherine Potmesil who began throwing pots there in the mid-1950s. They were give a state-wide award for their contributions and their plaque commemorating that award is on display with their pots. The Tom Jones Pottery in Clay City has a number of historical items on display including an old kiln. Tom Jones, who has been making pots for more than 40 years is still at work in Clay City about 10 miles east of Fairhope.

All this history and current pot making techniques are explained in a video that runs continuously at the Museum. Museum Director, Donnie Barrett, an authority on pottery, is always available to answer questions and bring the exhibits to life!

Curt Cochran, *Published in the Friends of the Fairhope Museum of History Vol. 5, Issue 3, June 2013*

Chapter 13

Petrified Indian Finger

The petrified Indian finger has been an enigma around Fairhope for years. Is it really as legend leads - from a Creek Indian, the loser in a battle with a Choctaw?

The finger appeared in Fairhope's first Museum, which opened in the late 1940's. That museum exhibited bizarre antiquities to attract sensational responses. It had skunks, snakes, birds in jars and stuffed animals of all kinds. There were also spears, an African mask, a German war helmet, a few flags and interesting guns. By the 1950's, children would dare each other to go in alone to look at, or even be close to, a shrunken head and the Petrified Indian Finger.

That first museum closed and the contents went into insecure storage. Most items were subsequently misplaced. The finger was sent to Fort Morgan in the 1960's, because that was the only museum in Baldwin County at the time. When Daphne opened its museum in 1974, the curator asked for their box of items back and not only received their items, but in the bottom of the box, was the petrified finger. When talk of a new Fairhope Museum began in 2002, residents who recalled the first museum asked, "Are we going to have the finger again?" Ms. Doris Allegri of Daphne recognized the appendage as belonging to Fairhope and returned it to Museum Director Barrett in 2008, when our current Museum of History opened.

The origin of the Finger was a mystery. First, was it real? Director Barrett took it to professional archaeologists at the University of South Alabama. They identified it as a real human finger by its grey color, fingerprint and porosity in the bone. And it was not from an American Indian, but from an Egyptian mummy!

Then, the question became, "How did it get here?". That answer is found not in Archaeology - but Sociology. From its outset in 1894, Fairhope's Single Tax Colony has been an interesting socio-economic experiment. Many of the curious visitors have always been academics and world travelers. Some had visited Egypt. Since the discovery of Egyptian King Tutankhamen's tomb in 1922, local entrepreneurs with more interest in money than in preserving their heritage have sold genuine and imitation antiquities. One of these travelers acquired the finger of a mummy. Just who brought it to Fairhope, and when, is not known. But the confirmed facts are that the original mummy finger was brought to this area and found its way into the Museum. But while the genuine finger is in the Fairhope archives, the appendage you see on display is a "reproduction" out of respect for it being an actual human body part. Although it is real, it isn't a petrified Indian "pinky". It is however a long-lasting piece of Fairhope history!

Bob Glennon, *Published in the Friends of the Fairhope Museum of History Newsletter Vol. 3, Issue 3, June 2012*

Chapter 14

Della Nichols – Fairhope's First Artist

Della Nichols – Fairhope's First Artist

Everyone who comes to Fairhope soon learns that it is an artist's haven that also attracts writers, musicians and other people with unique talents and abilities. It takes a while to learn that the first artist in Fairhope was actually here before Fairhope was founded. That artist was Della Nichols, who came with her husband in the summer of 1894. They arrived here and were waiting to welcome the Single Taxers.

Della Nichols, an accomplished artist from Shorter, Alabama, married Charles Edgar Nichols, when she was twenty-four years old. They acquired fifty acres of land on the Eastern Shore in the middle of what would become Fairhope, with the plan to build a house for themselves and twelve rental cottages. The house, called

"Liberty Castle", was built with three stories to give Della a third-story window where she could place a lantern so that Charles, the sea captain, could see it and find his way home in the dark.

This house was the only three-story house in Fairhope for a long time and remained the family home until the 1950s when it was sold to a developer to build the Bay Winds Condominiums. It was torn down in 1967. The cottages on the fifty acres known as Nicholasville were also sold and the name Nicholasville disappeared, as did the subdivision names of Adelville, Madelineville and Forrestdean. Nichols Ave. was named for the family. Liberty Street was named for the large elegant house.

Three generations of the family lived in Fairhope. Their one child, a son named Forest Edgar Nichols born in 1895, also became one of Fairhope's legends. He married and had two children, but was otherwise a rather helpless alcoholic. He died about a year before his mother, but the family kept it secret because of the property agreement in his divorce. The family just rolled him up in a blanket and put him "away". When Della died, the family announced that Forest had died and rolled him out of his blanket and had his funeral service with his mother. They were buried side-by-side.

Della was well known as an artist. Her favorite medium was painting on silk or satin which decays rapidly so very little of this work survived in good condition. She also did some painting on canvas, producing beautiful nature scenes, especially flowers. The centerpiece of her artwork that remains in the possession of her family is a large 6 ft by 6 ft quilt that has a variety of scenes and musical instruments, commonly called a "crazy quilt."

Fairhope

Most of her work remains as property of her family and hangs in their homes and rental cottages.

Della's great-granddaughter returned to Fairhope and began collecting and restoring Della's artwork. She agreed to put the art that she had on display at the Eastern Shore Art Center to celebrate the Fairhope Centennial in 1994. The artwork and family history was documented in the *Fairhope Courier* and other local newspapers during the Centennial year. It was a major part of the year long celebration in 1994.

Della's art was the first special exhibit of the Fairhope Museum of History when it opened in 2008. The photo on the previous page shows one of four paintings that was part of the Museum exhibit. The quilt was also on display.

Della Nichols continued with her art until her death in 1938. The few pieces that remain show her artistic talent and ability. Her long career as an artist gives some credence to the theory that it is the lovely location on the Eastern Shore that attracts artists and contributes to their creative energy. Fairhope is a very special place.

Curt Cochran, *Published in the Friends of the Fairhope Museum of History Newsletter Vol.6, Issue 6, December 2015 – January 2016*

Chapter 15

Stewart, the Picture Man

Frank Stewart, "The Picture Man," has done more than anyone to document the early history of Fairhope in pictures. His pictures are everywhere. Many are on display in the Fairhope Museum of History; many are in the books about Fairhope and some are still prized family possessions of Fairhope families. The Fairhope Museum has a collection of several hundred of his photos and many of them were on display as a special exhibit during the years 2009 and  2010. Everyone enjoys his pictures of historic Fairhope but few know about how he got to Fairhope or and how he produced all those photographs.

Frank Stewart was born into a large family in Indiana in 1855. His family moved to Kansas soon afterwards and spent the Civil War years there. His father was a political activist who played a role in forming the Lincoln Republican Party in Kansas. Not much is known about his early years although there is an urban legend that he was present for the Golden Spike ceremony of the Union Pacific Railroad in Utah in 1869, when he was 14 years old. At age 36, he was working for the C.R.I. & P Railroad in Chicago, as secretary to the president. That year, he married Ms. Harriet "Hattie" Gray. Like millions of others at the time, Stewart became enamored with the Single Tax theory and in the late 1890s decided to move to the vicinity of Fairhope to be part of the action. He found land cheaper outside of Fairhope and bought a forty-acre farm on Pole Cat Creek (which he called Silver Creek). By this time, he was an accomplished professional photographer using both glass plates and celluloid film and started his photography business right away, often traveling about in a horse-drawn buggy and later by car, while always carrying his heavy camera. In 1913, he gave up on the farm and moved into Fairhope to become an integral part of the city and the Single Tax experiment.

His Fairhope house and studio were on Section St. near the present-day Greer's Market. His photography studio was busy, but he still had time to go out photographing the Bay Boats, the People's Train, big celebrations and everyday life in Fairhope. He had a special camera which used celluloid film to make postcards, a popular item at the time. In the studio, he still used a glass plate camera for portraits because it could produce better quality pictures. Although he was 59 years old when he moved to Fairhope, he was able to climb to the top of the water tower in the center of town for pictures to record the development of the town. The first few years in Fairhope were his most active and he photographed just about everything. While there were other photographers in Fairhope who competed with him, none matched his variety or volume.

As more people were able to buy cameras and film, he went into film developing and printing pictures. Those who knew him, described him as a very formal man who was always well dressed. Family portraits in his studio were always a formal affair with his wife and niece getting people ready for pictures. Although he did have competition, he became the photographer that everybody wanted and remembered – Stewart the Picture Man. He worked on until 1936 when he sold the business – he was 81. His photographs remain a treasure for Fairhope.

Curt Cochran, *Published in the Friends of the Fairhope Museum of History NewsletterVol.6, Issue 5, October – November 2015*

Chapter 16

Fairhope's First Cartoonist - Bill Dealy

One-hundred and eighteen years ago, William A. Dealy moved to Fairhope and became well known locally as an artist. He is shown at his desk in the photo below, as a young man drawing cartoons. Mr. Dealy's focus was Fairhope, and his cartoons helped Fairhopeans learn to laugh at themselves and, perhaps, not to take themselves too seriously.

Dealy was born in Chicago in 1888 to Paul Kingston Dealy and his wife Adelaide. Kingston, an activist and spiritual leader, moved his family to Fairhope in 1898 to be part of the Single Tax movement. He was part of the Chicago Single Tax organization, which lavished some money, but also lots of criticism on Fairhope, in hopes of getting the Single Tax experiment to function the way *they* wanted.

The young Dealy who had a great talent for drawing and satire, soon began using both to highlight the many peculiar parts of Fairhope society and politics. At a young age, he began drawing cartoons about events in Fairhope and posting them on the city bulletin boards, which most residents in Fairhope checked at least once a day to see what was going on. He gave Marietta Johnson much of the credit for his career in art. He attended a professional art school after graduating from the Organic school.

Although later in Fairhope history Bill Dealy and his cartoons got most
 of the attention, the entire family was active in
Fairhope. Kingston is credited with bringing the
Baha'i Faith community to the South. The
community is still active in Fairhope and there
are several others in the Mobile area.

His first cartoons of Fairhope came to an end in
1916, when a hurricane destroyed his house. He
then decided to move his young family to Chicago. He eventually got a
job with the Army Corp of Engineers as an illustrator and with the
 Tennessee Valley Authority (TVA), living in
Florence, AL.

Most of his existing cartoons were drawn after he
retired and returned to Fairhope in 1948. Bill
Dealy was often described as a roustabout,
probably meaning that he did odd jobs besides his
cartoons.

The Fairhope Single Tax Corporation leaders were
a favorite subject, but he drew cartoons about all of Fairhope politics,
Fairhope eccentric characters, and important events in town. He also had
a serious side and drew illustrated maps of Fairhope which showed
details of streets, gullies and buildings.

Whenever something happened that
people talked about, you could expect
to see a Dealy cartoon posted on the
town bulletin boards. It was always
good for a laugh unless you were the

subject of his sketch. The cartoon on the left shows national FSTC leader
E.B. Gaston and implies that Fairhope was attracting Socialists,
Communists, Nudists, and Single Taxers, with the caption saying they
were all a bunch of Cranks. The cartoon on the right with the magnetized
horse shoe, also shows Fairhope attracting those with wild ideas. And
then there was Mayor Greeno. Dr. Greeno applied to become a member
of the FSTC twice but was turned down both times probably because he
was a leader of the "kickers" who wanted lower lease rates. He became

a strong anti-Single Taxer and started the rivalry between the city government and the FSTC. He was apparently a heavy drinker and rabble rouser, so Dealy drew him as straight laced. However, Dr. Greeno defeated Gaston in the first mayoral election in 1908. I guess you could say he got the last laugh.

Dealy drew most of the people of Fairhope at one time or another; one of his favorites was Mrs. Schramm, who lived in a tree house. The house was on Section St. just across from the present-day St. Lawrence Catholic Church. This cartoon [*right*], depicts her as the sexy Mae West. It was said that young boys would often watch her house hoping to see her come down to the ground level and get into her open-air bathtub. The house built on cut-off pine trees collapsed after she died.

New immigrants would often be the subject of Dealy cartoons, including the refugees from the Utopian colony in Ruskin, Georgia, or Dutch immigrants with "Van" in their name. The Ruskin colony was very socialist and collapsed first in Tennessee, then in Georgia. Many of the refugees' from Ruskin came to Fairhope and tried to turn the colony more socialistic. They were a factor in the revolt of the "Kickers" that eventually led to the establishment of the city government of Fairhope.

In later years, Dealy continued drawing and editing his Fairhope cartoons, and planned to publish a *Fairhope History in Cartoons*. He died in 1956 before it was published; however, many of his cartoons survive and are in the archives of our Fairhope Museum of History.

Curt Cochran, *Published in* the Friends of the Fairhope Museum of History Newsletter, *Vol. 7, Issue 1, February – March 2016*

Chapter 17

Ernest Berry Gaston
Fairhope's Ambassador to the Single Tax World

By 1926, the Single Tax movement in the United States was waning with only a few stalwarts, such as Fiske Warren, Bolton Hall and E. B. Gaston still promoting it as the answer to social problems. Several of the wealthier Single Taxers on the East Coast had created the Henry George Foundation to keep the Single Tax idea alive. The Foundation started holding annual Single Tax conferences. The 3rd annual conference, in 1926, was to be held in Copenhagen, Denmark starting on August 19th and E. B. Gaston decided to go.

The Single Tax community of Fairhope was very supportive, raising money to pay E. B. and Clara's travel expenses and gave them a grand Bon Voyage party as they started out at the end of July. On the way, E.B. and Clara stopped first, in Delaware to see the Arden and Free Acres Single Tax enclave, then on to Philadelphia to visit Henry George's past associates, including his editor, Mr. Louis F. Post. From there they went to Washington, D.C. to visit distinguished Single Taxers, including Colorado Representative Guy U. Hardy.

Last, they stopped in New York to visit Robert Schalkenbach. The Schalkenbach Foundation kept the works of Henry George and other Single Taxers in print. From New York, E. B. and Clara sailed to Copenhagen.

During the entire trip including the time aboard ship, E. B. wrote letters describing the travel, the people they met and their experiences, which were printed in the *Fairhope Courier*. From Copenhagen, he wrote about the city and culture and was particularly impressed by the number of bicycles and noted that any puff of wind would blow up the ladies skirts and dresses while they were pedaling.

In Copenhagen, E. B. and Clara were hosted by the Bjorner family, who were dedicated Danish Single Taxers. Mrs. Bjorner had actually visited Fairhope. The conference lasted three days and was attended by representatives from 17 countries. The Single Tax enclave's session on the evening of the 3rd day was hosted by Fiske Warren. He was well known for establishing Single Tax communities. E. B. gave a great presentation, which included 30 photographs, which were projected onto a screen as he gave his speech. The full text was later printed in the *Fairhope Courier*. He was delighted with all the favorable comments.

At the end, the conference organizers issued a number of pronouncements and also sent a recommendation to the League of Nations that all countries should implement a Land Value Taxation system.

On their return home, E. B. and Clara stopped in Philadelphia for the celebration of Henry George's 87th birthday and arrived in Fairhope on Sept the 9th, the day the Causeway was completed. This was E. B. Gaston's one and only trip abroad.

E. B. would continue to serve as the Secretary of the Fairhope Single Tax Corporation until 1936, when he installed his son, Corney, as the Secretary. E.B. died in 1937.

In the 1950s, E. B. Gaston's grandson, Paul, spend a year in Denmark and called on the same Bjorner family that hosted his grandfather.

They shared many stories about E. B.'s trip and declared that it was still a great time for the Single Tax Movement.

Curt Cochran, *Published in the Fairhope Museum of History Newsletter Vol. 7, Issue 4, August – September 2016*

Chapter 18

Adolph Berglin
The Ice Cream Man

I scream, you scream, we all scream for ice cream .. but did you know that the very first ice cream produced in the state of Alabama was right here in Fairhope? In 1897, an energetic young man came to Baldwin County from Wisconsin and immediately set to work as a self-employed entrepreneur, first as a vendor of fresh meat and other perishable foods, which he delivered from door to door with a horse-drawn wagon. This young man was Adolph Oscar Berglin, "A. O." to his friends.

As a dealer in perishables, A. O. recognized the need for ice, and soon thereafter, he leased a site on the beach from the Single Tax Colony. He established an ice plant there in 1918. The machinery and equipment consisted of mostly used items, assembly of which required all of his personal skills and mechanical abilities.

A steam boiler and engine furnished power for the operation with pine logs as fuel; thus, the cost of power was negligible. At the time, pine knots were available at no cost, from the cut-over open land. Steam power with wood fuel made it possible for the plant to pump its own water and produce its own electricity; it was almost self-sufficient. The two items coming from outside sources were salt and ammonia, both necessary for making ice.

Soon after the ice plant was placed in operation, milk and dairy processing equipment was added. When World War I brought shipbuilding and port activity to Mobile, *Fairhope Ice and Creamery Company* became a leading supplier of ice and dairy products. Especially popular were the ice cream cones and cantaloupe a-la-mode, sold to eager lines of customers on weekends. The beach was then crowded with summer residents and visitors who came to Fairhope via the Bay Boat excursions.

In 1915, A.O. developed his own business, and since he was mayor of Fairhope, his influence was also a key factor in planning the municipally-owned power plant and electrical distribution system. That utility has continually expanded and is now one of Fairhope's major assets.

Mr. Berglin also served as an officer of the Single Tax Corporation and member of its executive council for a number of years. He was also an original director of the Bank of Fairhope, a position he held throughout the remainder of his life.

So when you are enjoying your favorite flavor of ice cream, just remember where it all started .

Louie Blaze, *Published in the Friends of the Fairhope Museum of History Newsletter, Vol. 8, Issue 3, June – July 2017*

Chapter 19

Flo Simmons
Founder of Fairhope's Museum of History

Flo Simmons, one of Fairhope's great characters, accumulated an extensive collection of historical artifacts, photos, and stories that became the exhibits of the first Fairhope Museum of History when it opened in 1995. She had taken a class on how to operate a museum and was well known in the community; so that when people started discarding items of historical significance, they would give it to Flo instead. Her house overflowed with boxes. She was a leader of the founding committee that was formed in 1990 to establish the Museum.

The committee was able to secure the Bell Building on the Faulkner State College campus for the first Museum location which opened on a part time basis in 1995. Flo worked there as a docent three days a week until shortly before her death on Oct 13, 2005. The Bell Building didn't have room to display all of her collections. The Museum moved to its new location on Section Street in 2008 and has a large amount of Ms. Simmons' archive material.

Flora Maye Simmons, born in 1918, was the daughter of the well known Dr. & Mrs. Claude George Godard, Fairhope's most famous physician. Dr. Godard picked the name "Flora Maye" because it was the name of a Parisian perfume that he learned to like in France during WWI. (Dr. Godard apparently didn't spend all his war time in the trenches) She spent her entire life in Fairhope, becoming a bit of an eccentric. Besides discovery walks on the beach and nature exploration, she collected Indian artifacts and other unusual things to go along with her museum collections.

Her house in Fairhope at the corner of Mershon Street and Fairhope Avenue, has long been abandoned. The house was a gathering place for youngsters in the 1950s and 1960s and even Museum Director, Donnie Barrett, the same age as her son, William,

remembers hanging out there with young musicians practicing in the attached kitchen. Flo was always up for taking Fairhope youngsters on adventure trips or to a concert in her Nash Rambler station wagon with push button gears. Life changed for her in 1966 when her husband died of a heart attack and she had to move in with her aging parents to care for them. The house (photo above) has been vacant since she left, with the only use being as a haunted house for a few years. Those that remember Flo are getting fewer in number too, but her contributions to creating the Fairhope Museum of History will live on.

Curt Cochran, *Published in the Friends of the Fairhope Museum of History Newsletter, Vol. 6, Issue 4, August—September 2015*

Chapter 20

The Hermit of Montrose
"Poet of Tolstoy Park"

Tourists often come into the Museum and ask whether there is an exhibit on "The Poet of Tolstoy Park." They had obviously read the popular book by Sonny Brewer, a well-known Fairhope author, who made the house and the hermit famous. Unfortunately, there is no map. But Henry Stuart was real, and he did live in a round house on ten acres on the north edge of Fairhope that he named Tolstoy Park. He was a great admirer of Count Lev Nikolayevich (Leo) Tolstoy, Russian writer, philosopher and political thinker. Mr. Stuart had a beard, wore no shoes and was known to prefer privacy. Mr. Brewer's book is fiction, but it does accurately record what is known about Henry Stuart.

Mr. Stuart came to Montrose in 1923 from Idaho on the advice of his doctor to go to a warmer climate. The doctor suggested Southern California, but Henry chose Montrose instead. He was 65 years of age at the time and didn't expect to live very long – an apparent bad diagnosis. Nonetheless, he busied himself writing poetry, weaving tapestries and building his round block house, a marvel of building ingenuity. The house was ready for occupancy before the 1926 hurricane which was severe in the Mobile Bay area. It isn't clear whether he lived in the house all of the time, since he also retained the earlier building in which he lived while constructing the creative round structure.

Although his appearance made him look like a hermit, he was no recluse. He was more of a philosopher and was a long-time student and admirer of Tolstoy. With his Bachelor degree in Divinity and a lifetime of reading and study, he was well educated for the time. Stuart often had guests in his house, as indicated by his original guest book that had more than twelve-hundred signatures, including that of

Fairhope

Clarence Darrow, the civil liberties attorney famous for his defense in the Scopes "Monkey" Trial of 1925. There are several local newspaper stories which compared Stuart to Henry David Thoreau, another philosopher who lived similarly. He left Montrose in 1944 to return to his family in Oregon. He died about two years later.

Sonny Brewer arranged to rent and restore the block house while writing his book and often stayed in it. The book was published in 2005 and quickly became a best seller. The house is now open to the public with a new guest book signed by several thousand recent visitors to Tolstoy Park!

The round "Poet of Tolstoy Park" home of Henry Stuart is located north of downtown Fairhope, on the northwest corner of Parker Road and Highway 98, between the office buildings. Admission is free.

Curt Cochran, *Published in the Friends of the Fairhoope Museum of History Newsletter, Vol. 5, Issue 6, December 2014 – January 2015*

Chapter 21

Sam Dyson, Fairhope Businessman
Maybe Controversial – Always Interesting

Sam Dyson was one of the best known but controversial figures in the history of Fairhope. He was one of three sons of Marmaduke Dyson, who came to Fairhope in 1904. Marmaduke was an immigrant from Scotland who came of Philadelphia in the 1890s to start a new life. After hearing Henry George talk on his philosophy espoused in his book "Progress and Poverty," Marmaduke decided to come to Fairhope, AL to be part of the Single Tax demonstration. He and his wife had three sons; Raymond, George and Sam. They would all remain in Fairhope to the end of their lives.

Marmaduke and his sons had long careers as builders in Fairhope starting in 1911, in which they built many of the structures in downtown Fairhope. The building led to formation of the Dyson Construction Co (1952 – 1976) which was one of the largest construction companies in the Florida/Alabama panhandle when it was sold. The Dysons also ran a mercantile store for ten years. Sam was also the Chairman of the Board of the Fairhope National Bank from 1956 to '76. Sam was a proclaimed believer in the Single Tax theory and was an officer in the Fairhope Single Tax Corporation (FSTC) from 1956 to'76. Besides all his business interests, Sam supported the Organic School, was a Mason and a member of the Elks Club. The family's work and leadership are always noted in books on Fairhope (ie: *Fairhope 1894 – 1994*, *Images of American Fairhope*, and *A Fair Hope of Heaven*) which mostly show photographs of their buildings which are still seen across the city. Sam was also one of the accused in the notorious Mobile "Honor Killing" in 1932, and this may have slowed his business career somewhat.

Although the contributions were undeniable, Sam Dyson was a controversial figure in Fairhope. As head of the Fairhope National Bank he was said to use his position of power for political and other influence. He was president of the FSTC during the Rezner lawsuit, and was thought to be one of the leaders of the movement to disband the FSTC and re-incorporate it in the State of Delaware, which would make it more difficult to sue in Alabama. The effort was forbidden in the final Alabama Supreme Court decision on that lawsuit.

Although he was controversial, the city held a *Sam Dyson Day* on his birthday Feb 21, 1988, during which his many accomplishments were celebrated.

Some accomplishments were yet to come. In 1990, Sam self-published a short book on the history of Fairhope titled, *Fairhope – a*

Universal Community, which is still available in the city library. He also published a history of the Organic School and wrote many documents on the Single Tax for the Fairhope Single Tax Corporation.

Having become an expert on the History of Fairhope, Sam would come to the fledgling Fairhope Museum of History and offer his interpretation and opinion to the emerging Director Donnie Barrett, on the significance of exhibits and what should be said about them.

Sam died in 1998 as one of the unique personalities of Fairhope.

Curt Cochran, *Published in the Friends of the Fairhope Museum of History Newsletter, Vol 7, Issue 6, December 2016-January 2017*

Chapter 22

The Corte Family – Fairhope's Gatekeepers

Fairhope celebrated its centennial year in 1994 with a series of events throughout the year. As part of that celebration, the *Fairhope Courier* selected the Corte family as being the typical farmers near Fairhope.

The Corte family arrived in South Baldwin County in 1896. Over many years, they acquired 7500 acres of land just to the north of Fairhope stretching from Fly Creek at Mobile Bay on the west, beyond Hwy 27/181 on the east. The roads entering Fairhope from the north came through Corte land, so they became known as the gatekeepers.

The story of the Cortes of America began with Arturo Angelo (A. A.) Corte leaving his family home in the village of Valle de Cordo, in the Dolomite Mountains of north-east Italy, in 1887. He arrived in New York a few weeks later anxious to take advantage of the opportunities in the New World. The Italian migration to the U.S. was well underway and some 4 million Italians had immigrated by 1914. Opportunities in the U.S. were being scandalously promoted in Europe, but nonetheless, wages were about three times higher than in Italy and land was cheap in areas that were sparsely settled. Arturo was twenty-one years of age and anxious to make his fortune. The famous entry point for immigrants, Ellis Island, would not be established for a couple of years, so Arturo came through immigration processing at a facility called *Castle Garden*. He by-passed the Italian enclaves in the large cities and went to the iron ore mines in Michigan and later, Minnesota, where the wages were higher. He quickly settled into a frugal life of hard work to save money.

Working in the mines in Michigan, he met Allesandro (Alexander) Bertolla, another Italian Immigrant from the Dolomites. The legend is that the two of them decided they needed a cook and sent back to Italy for Alexander's sister, Magdalena to join them. She did. Magdalena and A.A. were married soon after she arrived and the Corte family of America began in 1889.

Madalena and A. A. Corte, seated, surrounded by their children.
Standing are: Julio, Adele, Ferdinand, Albert, Atilio, Ernest & Arthur

A.A. had worked in the mines for about six years when a real estate agent from South Alabama came through selling small plots of land in Baldwin County, Alabama. The man described Baldwin County so enthusiastically that A.A. bought a 10-acre farm just north of the new colony of Fairhope and moved his family in the spring of 1896. The Bertolla family would follow seven years later. The land was as good as advertised and they began clearing the land and farming. More children were added to the family to make a total of seven; six boys and one girl, by 1907. The boys helped with the farm work and sold their vegetables in Fairhope. They could often be seen in a mule-drawn wagon loaded with vegetables going down Fairhope Avenue and Mobile Street. The photo on the previous page shows the A. A. Corte family in the 1930s.

Money from selling vegetables and all other work was invested in more land. Baldwin county land was selling for about $1 per acre. The family formed the A. A. Corte and Sons Company and all seven of the children became partners in the business. By 1950, the company had become a major agri-business and the Cortes were very successful.

The major crops were Irish potatoes and "Silver Queen Corn," which required many laborers. They hired a variety of workers and offered temporary jobs to high school students in the area. Some older Fairhopeans remember going into the fields and digging potatoes all day in the hot sun. During the peak of the harvest season, the company shipped 100 rail car loads of potatoes and 20,000 boxes of corn each day. It was a massive operation! The Cortes lived on the land and enjoyed working together; often going to one of their homes for a family lunch for thirty or forty of them.

Ernest Corte built a house in Fairhope on Church St. in 1935 which remained a family home until the 1990s. It was offered to no avail, as the home for the Museum of History before it was demolished. Donnie Barrett, Director of the Museum, grew up on the Auburn Agricultural Extension and remembers the Cortes coming to presentations. There were many of them he recalled, and they always had a family gathering after the program. The Extension programs provided invaluable advice on how to efficiently grow crops and manage animals. The Cortes had large herds of Black Angus cattle.

The Alabama Corte family in 1994 at A. I. Corte Farm

They made a family photo in 1994, which shows the 3rd, 4th and 5th generations of this large family. Some of them still farm. Others are professionals, businessmen and real estate developers. The Cortes decided in year 2000 to write the story of the family. They went back to Italy to research their lineage and consequently, titled their story, *The A.A. Corte Family of Italy and America.*

As the third generation grew into adulthood, they began to migrate into other businesses or begin professional careers. Adele Corte was the last of the Corte children to run the company and did well into the 1970s. Teal Corte was the sales representative of the company that sold the most potatoes in the Southeast. As farming changed in the 1980s, The Corte and Sons Company business was closed and the assets divided among the family members. Corte Farms and Corte Land and Cattle Co. remain independent farming operations. The Corte name is now mostly associated with real estate developments in north Fairhope, with over 800 homes in *Rock Creek* built on Corte land. No other family has been as influential on the Eastern Shore.

Curt Cochran, *Published in the Friends of the Fairhope Museum of History Newsletter, Vol. 7, Issue 3, June – July 2016*

Chapter 23

Clarence Darrow - Fairhope's Celebrity Guest

Clarence Darrow is perhaps Fairhope's most famous visitor. He came to Fairhope to rest after the Scopes Monkey Trial in 1925. The trial got national attention through the reporting of famous journalist and avowed atheist, H. L Menken. Mr. Darrow had called the prosecuting attorney, and many times presidential candidate, William Jennings Bryan to the stand to testify as an expert on the Bible. Bryan's testimony and the trial in general, lacked the drama portrayed in the headlines and the movie and Darrow lost the case. The conviction was later reversed on a technicality. The trial had apparently been hard on both Bryan, who died five days later, and Darrow, who announced he would retire from his law practice in 1928 at age seventy. He is also remembered as a leading member of the American Civil Liberties Union.

Darrow visited Fairhope many times in the ensuing years and was often in the public eye. On one trip, he gave two speeches in Mobile talking about the poor treatment of black people and gave a similar speech in Daphne at the Baldwin County Training School, the Black high school. According to some news accounts, Darrow was sharply critical of how whites treated blacks. It was reported that private detectives were guarding Darrow in Mobile and circulars were distributed after his talk at the schools charging Darrow with "inciting ill feeling between negroes and whites." Other speeches were not so emotionally charge and were on a variety of subjects including "The Single Tax".

Darrow became a supporter of the Single Tax theory after reading Henry George's book "Progress and Poverty" and joined the Chicago Single Tax Club in the 1880s. This club, which was one of the largest in the country, took a great interest in Fairhope after it was founded in 1894.

Darrow explained his views on the Single Tax in a 1916 *Everyman* magazine article titled *"The Land Belongs to the People"* where he argued that the eminent domain laws should be used to appropriate the land for the people who lived and worked on it. In another article titled *"On Land and Labor"* he went even further to explain how unfair labor laws oppressed the workers. Darrow once made light of laws reducing labor hours by saying "the people liked to work so well that they had to have laws to stop them".

Darrow gave a great tribute to Henry George on the 75th anniversary of his birth in a speech to the Chicago Single Tax Club. George had died in 1897. That speech was taken from his lengthy article on Henry George in *Everyman* magazine which helped established him as great advocate for the Single Tax philosophy, although it was a slightly different version than Fairhope's.

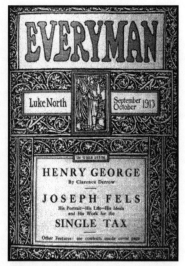

Mr. Darrow became quite an advocate of the Organic School and assisted Marietta Johnson with fundraising. He returned to Fairhope several times and traveled with Mrs. Johnson to promote the school. This continued into the next decade after his retirement. He died in Chicago on March 13, 1938 at 80 years of age.

Curt Cochran, *Published in the Friends of the Fairhope Museum of History Newsletter, Vol. 7, Issue 2, April – May 2016*

Chapter 24

Fairhope Golf is Older Than You Think

Twenty-one years, four months and two weeks after the Single-Taxers landed at Battles Wharf to establish Fairhope, the words "club," "driver" and "eagle" took on new meaning in the colony.

"Fairhope's new golf course will open tomorrow," announced the *Fairhope Courier* on March 17, 1916. Mr. Walter Fovargue, employed for eight months of the year as instructor of the Skokie Golf Club of Chicago, prepared plans in 1915 and came to Fairhope during his winter hiatus and laid out the 9-hole Fairhope course. The land for the course was set aside as a public park by the Fairhope Single Tax Corporation and "play upon it is under the control of the Fairhope Golf Club. The location is an easy walk from ... Mobile Bay", said the *Courier*. Excerpts from the newspaper stated that, "It winds through piney woods, with the shortest hole being (#2) 90 yards and the longest (#8), 266 yards. The tees and greens were made from red clay which has proven to be the best possible foundation. Few bunkers and hazards will be necessary, owing to the natural ability of the site chosen."

Prior to the course opening, the *Courier* proudly stated in it's February 11, 1916 Edition that "A suite of rooms occupied by a family of six, rented last week for the season at one of these places for $186 a week, just because of the golf course.". Golf fees advertised on March 31, 1916 were $10 for the season or $.50 a day.

Seven years later, an article in the *Fairhope Courier* [*January 5, 1923*] said it all began in 1916 with the Fairhope Golf, Gun and Country Club, which was the "focal point of golf and social life in our community."

The club house was built in 1922 and still stands today off Johnson Street, one block south of Fairhope Avenue, a quarter-mile east of the current Fairhope Post Office. The building, now a home, is leased from the

Fairhope Single Tax Corporation by Delbert and Roberta Long. The short article in the *Courier* cited that "Members of the Fairhope Gun and Country Club dedicated their beautiful new club house with a delightful dance Monday, New Year's night. There were about 50 people present."

The Original Fairhope Golf, Gun and Country Club

The public park designated for the course, was located between Fairhope & Morphy (north-south) Streets and Mershon and Ingleside (east-west) Streets. The course was closed in the late 1950's when the land was returned to the Single Tax Colony for housing development. Perhaps the stress of not having a town golf course was lightened by the fact that the Grand Hotel at Point Clear opened two 9-hole golf courses in 1947. It later added two more 9-hole courses.

In 1985, there was a frail attempt to again bring golf back to Fairhope. *The Mobile Register* in January 1985 noted that the Fairhope Recreation Board had authorized $15,000 to fund conceptual plans for an 18-hole golf course in Fairhope; on land to be donated by Angelo Corte, Fred Corte and Madeline Berglin. This was 150 acres "off highway 98 between Parker Road and Gulf Coast Substation." (sic). But six developers did not exercise their option to buy *[part of 400 acres of]* land from Corte; thus negating the free land offer to the city. But this didn't end the campaign by area golfers to get another course.

In April 1985, a goal was set to raise $650,000 to $1,000,000 by June 1 in order to show support for construction of a course at Highway 104 and U.S. 98. By June of that year, $1.1 million had been pledged and committed. A minimum monthly fee of twenty-five dollars was set for memberships, to remain in effect for the first three years that the course was open.

But in July 1985, *The Mobile Press-Register* reported that the Fairhope City Council voted to scrap all plans to construct the 18-hole course on donated land and return all funds designated for the project by July 31 of that year.

Construction cost exceeding budgeted funds was the reason given for canceling plans on the Corte/Berglin donated land. City Councilman Barney Shull, with encouragement from local golfers, said they would continue to look for an 18-hole course site. A local un-named builder told the City Council that he would build the course if he could get a $1 million pledge of support from the residents. The developer wanted to build the course between Greeno Rd and Section Street. But soon thereafter, the developer's bank [also not named] decided that Fairhope was too small to sustain the course and backed out of financing the venture.

Councilman Shull once again took up the task of stirring interest, this time for a $1 million General Obligation Bond. "Season pass sales were overwhelming before the first shovel full of dirt was dug," said the *Eastern Shore Courier,* dated July 4, 1990, reflecting back on the 1986 funding effort. Encouraged by that support, the city bought 150 acres from Dr. O.O. Jones and Matt Dial east of the city off County Road 27; now State Highway 181.

A few months later, the city bought an additional fifty acres in order to someday add another 9 holes. Mr. Shull, an engineer for the Army Corp of Engineers, helped design the course and the city hired Horace W. Smith, who had built many courses around the Southeast, for the construction work. Smith completed the task in May, 1987. On April 4, 1988, the Fairhope 18-hole Golf Course at Quail Creek opened with Harry Dyer as the Course Professional. The Quail Creek Estates Sub-division was built around the perimeter of the course.

On opening day, the cost to play a round of 18 holes was $9. The 6500-yard course hosted over 200 golfers that first day. Several tournaments were scheduled immediately and the full service course with Pro Shop, driving range, snack shop and equipment rentals was a hit from the start. On August 19-20, 1989, the Mayor's golf tournament was held at the course. Local professional golfer Bobby Hall joined the city staff in January 1989 and continues today as the club professional.

Fairhope golf got another attractive boost in 1993, when the 18-hole Rock Creek Golf Course was opened. Private developers David Head and Kenny McLean turned land east of Hwy 98 north of downtown Fairhope into the Rock Creek Community of about 1000 homes. The land was also previously owned by Greek settler, A. Corte, who began buying land along Rock Creek in 1876. It had been his descendants who offered land to the Fairhope Recreation Board in 1985.

Falkner State College uses Rock Creek as the home course for its golf team. Contemporary professional golfer Bubba Watson, played the course when he attended Faulkner and is still remembered by some Rock Creek players.

Now, within minutes of downtown Fairhope, Rock Creek, Lakewood (Grand Hotel) and Quail Creek Golf Courses offer golfers superb choices for challenging outings.

Fairhope's Quail Creek Golf Course is an affordable, city-owned course, three miles east of downtown. The course includes well manicured greens, fairways, tee boxes, a full-service Pro Shop and a friendly & knowledgeable staff.

Jim Bates, Assistant Director of the Fairhope Museum of History and avid golf enthusiast, (pictured here) says, "We are fortunate to have so many great courses on the Eastern Shore, but our Fairhope Quail Creek is the most challenging course of them all. We can proudly consider ourselves a 'golf destination'!"

Bob Glennon, *Published in the Friends of the Fairhope Museum of History Newsletter, Volume 4, Issue 5, October – November 2013*

Chapter 25

Fairhope's Colonial Inn

The Overton family of Fairhope, the one-time owners of the Colonial Inn, found a treasure in their attic! - An old scrapbook and photo album. The photos had baked for years in the hot storage area and newspaper clippings were crumbling. Yet, the album contained a wealth of information about life in Fairhope through the eyes of the guests at the Colonial Inn. Thanks to their generosity, those data are now a part of our Museum collection.

The Colonial Inn was the finest luxury hotel in Fairhope when it was built in 1909 by the Sacriste sisters: Vienna McClintock and Ann Morgan. Fairhope attracted tourists from the very beginning and became widely known as a very special place, attracting visitors from all over. By the 1920s, wealthier visitors came from Chicago, Detroit, Milwaukee and other large Eastern cities to spend a few weeks or months during the winter and to enjoy the climate and Southern lifestyle. The Colonial Inn provided excellent food, attentive service, entertainment, parties and a great view of Mobile Bay.

The information in the scrapbook/album comes mostly from those guests who after returning to their homes, would write letters to the Inn describing what a great time they had during their stay and including pictures, poems and stories. The *Fairhope Courier* would print their comments with the pictures, in a regular *Courier* column, "Colonial Inn News."

The entertainment for the Colonial Inn guests included dinner music with local musicians, poetry readings in the evenings, plays which were usually put on by the guests themselves and of course parties. The Sacriste sisters were great entertainers. The new Colonial Inn exhibit features pictures of people in costume at a "patent medicine party", where the party-goers dress as their favorite medicine. It shows some insight into the culture of the 1920s when patent medicines were very popular. Another photo shows guests dressed as pirates in a treasure hunt, looking for planted clues. Pictures and descriptions of many other parties, the various guests and life in Fairhope are contained in the many pages of the album. The glory days of the Colonial Inn documented in the album were from about 1916 to 1930. The national personalities who visited Fairhope and stayed at the Inn during that time included educator John Dewey, actor Robert Smith, presidential candidate and New York Mayor Al Smith and famous attorney Clarence Darrow.

The Great Depression of October 1929 initiated a decline for the Inn. In the 1940s, other newer hotels opened to serve the influx of people into Mobile's shipbuilding industry during WWII. This created more competition. The decline continued until the Colonial Inn closed in 1992 and the building was demolished.

Curt Cochran, *Published in* the Friends of the Fairhope Museum of History Newsletter, *Vol. 4, Issue 6, December 2013 – January 2014*

Chapter 26

The Museum Fire Truck

Housed in the Fairhope Museum of History in retirement amongst a collection of vintage fire equipment, helmets and the like is a 1934 Ford Fire truck (plate 1935) powered by the venerable 85 HP Ford flathead V8 made famous by Bonnie and Clyde. Beautifully restored and lovingly maintained, the truck belonged to the Fairhope

 Volunteer Fire Department and has a long history.

Built by the Peter Pirsch Company of Kenosha, WI, the Pirsch Company was the pre-eminent fire truck manufacturer of its day. The company was founded by Peter Pirsch in the early 20's and rolled out its last truck in 1987. The Fairhope truck started its working life in 1935 in the small town of Hogansville, GA (population about 2300 now) which is located near Warm Springs GA, where President Franklin Roosevelt often visited for treatment for his polio and where he later died.

The Pirsch built truck was ordered on a Ford chassis, reportedly at the behest of the local Hogansville Ford dealer who was also servicing the open Ford convertible with hand controls used by President Roosevelt. The Pirsch Company built many engines on different frames depending on buyer preference. The Hogansville truck was a 500-gallon Pumper of the open cab variety. It was purchased by

Fairhope from Hogansville in 1954 and while the actual purchase price seems lost to history, a good estimate using price guides keyed to the time would be in the neighborhood of $3000-3500 equipped.

Private contributions from residents of the Eastern Shore were solicited to purchase the truck. While Fairhope had another fire truck (a 1946 model), if it was out responding and another call came in, the Eastern Shore down to Mullet Point was basically without protection. The used truck performed faithfully in service to Fairhope but it was no picnic to drive. The truck did not have power steering; it had mechanical brakes and a manual shift transmission with a heavy truck clutch. Bringing the truck to a halt with firemen on the back plus a full 500-gallon water tank (about 5000 lbs right there) required huge mechanical effort, no small measure of prayers, and that the brakes be adjusted virtually on a daily basis! It would also be important to know the mechanics of "double clutching" to use engine back pressure to help in stopping. The truck is only driven for ceremonial occasions today and is not for the faint of heart to undertake.

According to Tom Odom who now serves as the City Fire Inspector and who worked the truck after arriving in 1953, the city's first fire station was downtown on Section Street, at the site of the current city Welcome Center. At the time, the building also housed the police department and the generating plant for the city-owned utilities. Odom says fire fighters were alerted by a siren. As soon as three men arrived in response, they grabbed the slickers and went off to respond. Most common calls were house and grass fires. The truck was physically housed in a metal building to the rear of what is now the Visitor Center where there was also a large water tank and the diesel engines for Fairhope utilities. A far cry from the pampered air-conditioned quarters our truck enjoys today!!!

Dr. Ralph Thayer, *Published in the Friends of the Fairhope Museum of HistoryNewsletter, Vol 2, Issue 4, August 2011*

Chapter 27

Fairhope Monopoly Board

Fairhope street names appearing on an early Monopoly game Board opposite New York City is an interesting part of its early history as a Single Tax Colony.

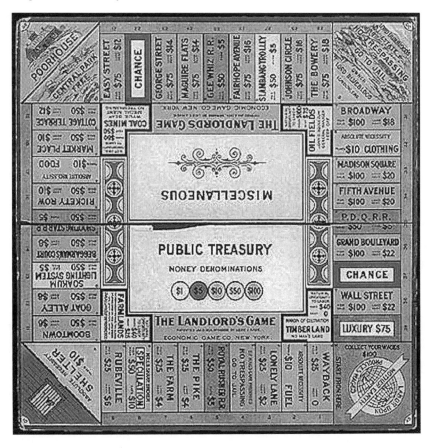

The photo is of the Arden Board, one of the very earliest versions of the game which featured Fairhope Avenue, Johnston Circle and George St. as primary locations on the board along with Wall St,

Broadway and Madison Square. The Board is the familiar Monopoly type layout but was called the Landlord's game, the name given it by Lizzie Magee a professional game designer who obtained the first patent on the game in 1904. She was a Quaker and strong supporter of the Single Tax principle advocated by Henry George. She, like tens of thousands of others who were members of Single Tax clubs throughout the country, would have known about Fairhope as a Single Tax experiment. When she got the patent for the Landlord's Game she was living in the Single Tax Colony of Arden, Delaware, thus the name Arden Board.

The Arden Board was one of several versions she created to try to generate more interest in the board game and to sell more of them. The board, included with the 1904 patent, did not have street names but a tax of specific value on the board locations. The original game has two sets of rules with one set showing the virtues of the single tax approach to land ownership and the other, the normal private ownership. She developed the game to teach the virtues of the single tax principle by showing the evils of land speculation and how the single tax on land values was a better approach to prosperity for all.

She renewed her patent on the Landlord's Game in 1924 to try to maintain control of the game. The second board added the Fairhope street name Fels Avenue. Joseph Fels was a wealthy Philadelphia man who contributed extensively to Fairhope in support of the Single Tax Experiment. By this time, other individuals had developed and published similar board games with different names such as Fortune, Money and Real Estate. None of these Monopoly type games became widely popular mostly because their creators were unable to interest the large game publisher Parker Brothers in publishing and marketing them. Parker Brothers had published other games written by Lizzie Magee but they considered the Landlord's Game unsatisfactory because it had to many rules and took to long to play.

In the early 1930s, an unemployed salesman in Germantown, PA named Charles Darrow developed a similar board game using street names in Atlantic City and New Jersey like Park Place, Marvin Gardens, Baltic Ave., etc. and called it "Monopoly." Darrow was able to convince Parker Brothers to publish the game through a family connection to one of the Parker Brothers' executives.

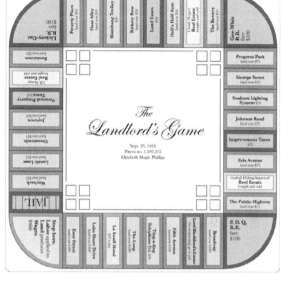

The Monopoly game published in 1935 became an instant hit selling by the tens of thousands.

Lizzie Magee's 1924 patent for the Landlord's Game. Fels Ave. is added and Fairhope Ave. is not there.

Darrow was paid royalties and became a millionaire; Parker Brothers had their most successful board game ever. With the success of the Monopoly game, Parker Brothers became concerned about intellectual property rights and did a patent search. They found at least three existing patents that they decided they had to address. Lizzie Magee's was one of those. She accepted five hundred dollars for her rights to the two patents that she had filed. Some historians write that she was happy with this deal since she thought it would publicize the Single Tax principle. Two other patent lawsuits were settled for many thousands of dollars. The lawsuits continued for many years as the Monopoly game sold by the millions.

Although other similar games were created, Monopoly remained by far the most popular. Atlantic City street names became known to millions and Fairhope Ave. to only a few. A Monopoly 50th

Fairhope

Anniversary magazine article stated that Atlantic City and the streets made famous by Monopoly were in decline and pretty run down.

Fairhope of course, is doing just fine.

Curt Cochran, *Published in the Friends of the Fairhope Museum of History Newsletter, Volume 5, Issue 2 April – May 2014*

Chapter 28

Farragut enters Mobile Bay - August 5, '64

The ships were dressed from stem to stern in flags, as if for a gala day, and every man sprang to his station when the roll called, "All hands to general quarters." It was twenty minutes to six in the morning and day was just beginning to break. Eighteen Federal ships moved at "low steam" past the Sand Island bar into the channel entering Mobile Bay. Suddenly out of the southeast, the *Red Gauntlet* swept into hazy view. In another twenty minutes, this sleek gray, almost invisible side-wheel steamer designed to outrun almost any ship of its time, would slip safely into the bay. This blockade runner was ending a voyage of seven thousand miles without incident. There was a west wind and flood tide. At 6:47 a.m., a puff of smoke appeared from the lead ironclad and the day became an historic milestone – the beginning of the Federal attack on Fort Morgan. The Battle of Mobile Bay had begun.

The Union ships, including four ironsides, began their attack on Fort Morgan, as four Confederate warships, with one ironclad, waited in the bay. Near Fort Gaines on Dauphin Island, Federal land troops had advanced to within 1,700 yards of Fort Gaines. By 10 a.m., the battle was over. The Confederate Ram, *CSS Tennessee*, the most formidable warship in the Southern fleet, was compelled to surrender. CSS Admiral Buchanan was so seriously wounded that Union Admiral Farragut sent his regrets and offered anything in his power to help. Buchanan only requested that his "fleet-surgeon" and his aides be allowed to accompany him wherever he might be sent, until recovered from his wound. Confederate General Page at Fort Morgan, allowed under flag of truce, for the *U.S.S. Metacomet* to take Buchanan and other wounded Confederate sailors to the Union hospital at Pensacola, where they could receive "more comfortable quarters than we can give in the fleet." This humanitarian gesture characterized the virtues of gentlemen in this War Between the States.

This formidable event occurred 150 years ago. The acrid odor of gunpowder and the thunder of Brooke rifles and Dahlgren cannon, stirred wildlife that morning as it grazed on the bluff that would become Fairhope, thirty years later.

Bob Glennon, *Published in the Friends of the Fairhope Museum of History Newsletter, Vol.5, Issue 4, August 2014*

Chapter 29

The Battle for Mobile – April '65

Thirty-two thousand of the 43,000 Federal troops to later participate in the Battle for Mobile, had gathered and camped for three weeks at Dannelly's Mill on Fish River in south central Baldwin County. The Civil War had waned on for four years. Most thought it would last less than a year. Forts Gaines, Powell and Morgan that had gallantly fortified the entrance to Mobile Bay, fell eight months before, but the U.S. fleet had been unable to approach the city of Mobile due to defenses and obstructions placed in the shallow bay. Mobile was the last seaport to remain open even though the blockade of Federal ships had inhibited all but the boldest of blockade runners. Even that was now stopped since the bay was occupied by Federal gunboats. This city that thrived by the sea would be attacked by land. Foot soldiers coming overland from Pensacola and those staged in Baldwin County were closing in on Spanish Fort and Blakeley. Spanish Fort and Fort Blakeley were manned and ready, with 4000 Confederates defending their pride. For the Federals, it was a mission to restore the United States. For the South, it was protecting the farm and life style.

The 150th Anniversary of the battles to claim Mobile is at hand this April 2015. The confrontation began on March 27 and ended April 12, 1865. It was the final decisive battle of the War Between the States and the city of Mobile was abandoned by the Confederate defenders on the nights of April 10th and 11th to avoid the cannonade that had the might to destroy Mobile.

Fairhope wasn't a settlement yet, but Volanta and Alabama City were small villages of potters and farmers who offered no threat to the encroaching army. Most local men were away serving the

Confederacy, leaving the Eastern Shore to the local militia and limited number of Southern defenders. The women and children bravely stood their ground to protect their property, but the army was conspicuously dominant. Being in an "occupied" land was bizarre. Federal troops marched past homesteads on civilian roads prior to the forthcoming siege. Some were hostile while some were polite. One could not tell which, until they were face-to-face. A U.S. Illinois regiment respectfully asked permission to spend the night in the Union Church in Daphne and permission was granted, provided they would leave it as they found it. And they did. At other times, hungry troops confiscated food, crops and animals from defenseless owners or poked bayonets and pitchforks into the yards and flowerbeds of homes, searching for buried family treasures and silverware.

Nothing about the invasion was pleasant or desired, by either side. The aggressors were far from home and didn't want to be here, except for their military mission. The defenders just wanted them on the other side of the line. Even humanitarian acts to aid the wounded, or feed the weak, were simultaneously lauded and drew anger.

On April 9, the gunfire stopped, but all wasn't well. Every family in America had been affected in severe ways. For the next 150 years,

historians and outdoorsmen would pick up spent lead bullets, iron projectiles, uniform buttons and memorabilia - all reminders of the War. Mothers became grandmothers and great-grandmothers with sad memories of sons and husbands who had given their best for their country.

Baldwin County did not go unscathed. The last major battle of the Civil War was fought within ear-shot of our Museum. Somehow… it all wasn't worth it.

Bob Glennon, *Published in the Friends of the Fairhope Museum of History Newsletter, Vol. 5, Issue 3, June 2013*

Chapter 30

Pioneer II - Prototype Confederate Submarine

The April 18, 1864, headline that the Federal warship *USS Housatonic* had been sunk in Charleston harbor was a morale building event for the Confederacy. The Confederate submarine *CSS Hunley* that sank the *Housatonic,* had been shipped from Mobile by rail, arriving in Charleston, S.C. on August 12, 1863. *Park and Lyons Machine Shop* on Water Street in Mobile was the manufacturer.

The clandestine work on a subsurface warship by Horace Hunley, James McClintock and Baxter Watson in New Orleans was aborted on April 25, 1862, when U.S. Admiral Farragut "ran the gauntlet" past two Mississippi River forts and captured New Orleans. Historical documents show that a prototype submarine, the *Pioneer*, was tested in 1862 in Lake Pontchatrain, but the "fish boat" was scuttled when Union ships converged on the city. Hunley, McClintock & Watson moved to Mobile, joined Thomas Park and Thomas Lyons and began developing another submarine, *Pioneer II.* Some historic documents cite the name as *American Diver*; either or both are possible. The vessel began sea trials in January 1863 and an attempt was made to assault the Union blockade off Dauphin Island in February 1863, but the effort failed. The submarine is said to have been lost in the bay or outside the mouth in the Gulf.

Construction of the CSS *Hunley* began here in Mobile immediately after the loss of *Pioneer II.* It was tubular, 4 feet tall, forty feet long and designed for a crew of eight: seven to turn the hand-crank propeller and one to

Park and Lyons Machine Works, Mobile

steer and direct the boat. It contained ballast tanks to descend and hand-pumps to surface. It was tested in the Mobile River and Mobile Bay. By July 1863, the *Hunley* demonstrated its potential by "attacking" a coal flatboat in Mobile Bay. The test was supervised by Confederate Admiral Franklin Buchanan, later to be the commander of the *CSS Tennessee* in the Battle of Mobile Bay. The submarine *Hunley* was acquired by the Confederate States of America and put into service on February 17, 1864. It disappeared that night. On August 8, 2000, it was found in Charleston harbor.

There is some speculation that the *Pioneer II* or *American Diver* are lying covered with mud beneath the waves of Mobile Bay, or outside in the Gulf. There have been twenty-seven documented searches granted by the state to find these trophies since 1995. Nothing of consequence has been found.

The interest continues as accounts by men who worked on the vessel(s) commented about their experience: Lt. William A. Alexander, an engineer in the 21st Alabama Infantry, assisted with the design and construction of the submarine. He later wrote that "it was towed off Fort Morgan intending to man it and attack the blockading fleet outside, but the weather was rough and with a heavy sea, the submarine became unmanageable and finally sank, but no lives were lost." The Subs' machinist, James McClintock wrote, "To obtain room for the machinery and five persons, she was built thirty-six feet long, three feet wide and four feet high; twelve feet at each end was built tapering to make her easy to pass through the water."

The iron hull's ability to evade seekers is due to murky water limiting visibility to about four to six feet and hampered by years of sediment and dredging. The construction of the Cochran Bridge Causeway in 1927 has caused the once-forty-foot-channels of the Blakely, Apalachee, Tensaw, Spanish and Mobile Rivers to deposit silt in the bay leaving it only four to six feet deep in places. The commercial ship channel has also been dredged to fifty-five feet. Marine archeologists have searched waters from nine to forty-six feet throughout the bay, with the most promising areas being in or around the outer ship channel. There are also strong arguments for "right at the docks" on the Mobile River, but surely dredging would have revealed anything there by now. Neither location is practical for "recreational diving" among ships' propellers.

It is noteworthy in our history, that some of this first submarine testing was done in Baldwin County waters where forty years later, the bay boat *Fairhope* would ply its way into the city.

Bob Glennon, *Published in the Friends of the Fairhope Museum of History Newsletter, Vol. 7, Issue 1, February – March 2016*

Chapter 31

Submarine Spotted in Mobile Bay Near Fairhope

September, 1942 - While on the subject of World War II, it is noteworthy that a German Submarine was spotted this week offshore Fairhope by 10 year old Lila Pennington and her two siblings, Buddy, eight and Wilma, twelve, while playing on the beach near sundown. The attack on Pearl Harbor on December 7 has everyone on edge and evidently according to these citizens, for good reason. The Pennington children called their father, "Capt. "Penny" Pennington, the owner of a seafood shop on Section Street, and he too saw the silhouette of the submersible watercraft; "probably 400 yards off the beach," said brother, Buddy. Ms. Pennington said that it appeared to be a small one-man German submarine. The craft flashed a light in the direction of Fly Creek and a return signal was flashed back from that area. Neither the civilian shore patrol, nor city police were able to apprehend anyone involved.

April 2012 - Mrs. Pennington Ryals, now in her late '70's, who visits the Fairhope Museum of History periodically, recently confirmed again to the Museum Director, that she did indeed see the craft.

In an effort to verify the sighting, the *Friends* Newsletter contacted Dr. Michael Thomason, Director Emeritus of the University of South Alabama Archives, on February 28, 2012, on the matter. The Professor is quoted as saying that the appearance of a submarine in bay waters was highly unlikely due to the insufficient water depth needed for a submersible to operate, particularly near the Eastern Shoreline. "How would it get here?" he asks. "It would have to be transported all the way from Germany."

While few sightings have been confirmed in this area, by either Mr. Snook's Gulf Telephone Company Civil Patrol, or the U.S. Coast Guard, all Lookouts are urged to be on Alert in view of this event. Any unfamiliar activity should be reported to the Operator or to the Police Chief.

The facts of this story were reported by Staff Writer, Mike Odom in the "Gulf Coast Newspapers" on August 19 – 20, 2009.

Bob Glennon, *Published in the Friends of the Fairhope Museum of History Newsletter, Vol 3, Issue 2, April 2012*

Chapter 32

LITTLE KNOWN FACT "DUG UP" UNDER THE MUSEUM

One of the pleasant advantages as a docent in the Fairhope Museum of History is the privilege of learning from the exhibits historical facts and curiously interesting stories. Sometimes a seemingly insignificant piece of an exhibit can spark the curiosity to force further study into that history. This curiosity led me to question the reason for the exhibited piece of bent iron identifying it as a piece of rebar "from the Civil Defense shelter that once existed below the museum." To heighten my curiosity, Donnie Barrett, director of the museum, told me that the shelter was converted from an underground water storage tank which provided a water system serving the city in the early days of Fairhope. Wow! That amazed me even more and I felt compelled to *dig further into that underground mystery*. As I began to mention this to a few "old timers," I found that only a few were able to give me the information I was seeking. Thus began my adventure in researching this secret mystery. Since it all started with Donnie's information, though sketchy as it was, he suggested some folks that I might question to get to the bottom of the underground structure. Herein lays my tale of history.

It began shortly after the 1894 date when the founders arrived and began making a town for themselves. Probably their biggest need was a supply of fresh water. The nearest fresh water was several miles south of town at Sweet Water Branch. The town supplied a wagon loaded with barrels to collect that water and bring it back to the city. This horse-drawn wagon-load of water was also to be used for future fire-fighting, if necessary. Its initial call to action, however, ended catastrophically. The crowd of anxious volunteer fire fighters rushed to the wagon with such exuberance, the horses were startled into running wildly up the street as far north as the cemetery where the wagon ended in wreckage and the water lost.

Around the year 1897, a well was drilled in the center of town, now the intersection of Fairhope Ave. and Section St., and a hand pump was installed. A gentleman named C. L. Coleman master minded the project and funded it with his own money. This was the beginning of Fairhope's water department which continued to grow. In 1915 a "modern" steel water tower was erected behind what later would become City Hall, now the Fairhope Museum of History. This water tower was replaced in 1935.

My research took me to a number of long time Fairhope folks, most of whom knew nothing about a bomb shelter, let alone an underground water tank. Then I was introduced to Mr. Tom Odom. Mr. Odom, who came to Fairhope to organize the National Guard unit in 1953, recalls that there was indeed an underground water purification system that was located behind City Hall (now the Museum) and was part of the system that provided the city with water. The reservoir was a large metal tank with a screened roof to keep out litter as well as provide an escape of fumes from the chemicals used to purify the water. Water was pumped from a well operated by electricity from the generating plant located in the building next door, a site on which later was built the Welcome Center. The water tower built in 1915 became the city water department providing water right to the homes. Thus began the Fairhope Water Department which has become the largest supplier of water in Baldwin County, with five water towers pumping millions of gallons of water each day. So, what became of the water tank?

"DUCK AND COVER"

With the 1950s came the threat of enemy attack and the cold war with USSR. Our government's attempt at protecting its citizens was to urge us all to build our own bomb shelters.

"THE BEST WAY TO SURVIVE THE HAZARDS OF RADIOACTIVE FALLOUT, OR ANY OTHER THREAT AN ENEMY MAY USE AGAINST US, IS TO BE PREPARED - - KNOW THE FACTS -- LEARN WHAT TO DO, NOW!"

This was the message that appeared on 1950s posters. *"DUCK AND COVER!"* These words reflected an abiding national concern with civil defense that reached as far back as to the Minutemen, spread nationwide during World War II, and rose and fell with the tensions of the Cold War. Ranging from home-made dirt-covered shelters to commercially-fabricated ones, shelters became a national obsession during the '50s. Recommended by national Office of Civil Defense, a typical fallout shelter would include a fourteen day food supply which may be stored indefinitely, a battery-operated radio, auxiliary light sources, a two-week supply of water, first aid, sanitary and other miscellaneous supplies and equipment.

Fairhope was not to be left behind in this endeavor to protect its citizens and decided to do what was necessary to protect the city government from a dreaded nuclear attack, and city officials took wise and careful steps in that direction. With federal and city dollars, the safe chamber was constructed by converting that abandoned water tank (already underground) into a safe shelter. With very careful and detailed research and thorough and comprehensive planning the Civil Defense shelter became a reality. Holes were cut into the walls of the tank providing the entrance as well as stairs built leading downward into the interior. Steel bars reinforcing eighteen-inch-thick concrete walls and ceiling would serve as the required defense against enemy bombs. Fortunately for all, the shelter was never needed against bombing and because of its proximity to City Hall, it became an adjunct to the Police Department.

WELCOME FREDERICK

Fast forward to the 1979 hurricane season: now with unlimited electricity, the chamber had been converted to the "Emergency Operations Center" making it available to the city government in the event of a perilous situation. Modern communication equipment was installed as well as furnishings which would accommodate any who would seek refuge. According to retired member of the police department Mike Randall, the shelter was accessed through doors on the north side with four steps leading downward to a center hallway. To the left of the hall were four sets of bunk beds opposite "cubby holes," offices furnished with desks and chairs as well as a bank of radio equipment. At the end of the hall was a small but well-equipped kitchen and across the hall was a rest room. Officer Randall remembers at times that the space was filled with bicycles that had been abandoned and stored there until Christmas when they were given away. Besides serving as general storage space, it was also used at times for interrogation of prisoners by the police department.

Hurricane Frederick's arrival in September 1979 offered a good excuse to put the "EOC" to use. Shirley Nolte Davenport, daughter of former police chief Nolte, tells of spending that night with her family in the shelter to escape the possible ravages of the category three storm. "It was a little room, painted drab green, with bunk beds where we spent the night. Radio and TV equipment occupied a large counter that was separated from the bunk beds area by a concrete partition which limited our view of the TV to only one spot on one of the beds. The entrance was a thick metal door which led downward some steps." Again, with the impending danger of another dangerous hurricane, Danny in 2003, it was considered to be the "shelter from the storm." However, upon inspection standing water and the general condition made it unsuitable for use.

HISTORY STRIKES AGAIN

Fast forward again to 2007. When the building site for the extension of the museum was determined, the existing underground chamber would have to be dealt with. The proposed two-story building of about six thousand square feet needed an adequate foundation instead of a concrete-walled hole in the ground. Heavy demolition equipment and expertise went to work to remove the walls of iron and concrete and to fill in the space needed for the foundation of the new building.

The thick concrete walls and ceiling were demolished - no easy task with conventional bulldozing equipment. Donnie Barrett remembers a giant wrecking ball and battering rams employed to crash in the roof, causing the entire structure to be crushed into itself. Onlookers recalled that the site's twisted steel bars resembled huge amounts of iron spaghetti.

THE MYSTERY ENDS

Before demolition began, a curious inspection of the shelter took place where some supplies remained. Museum director Donnie Barrett was one who descended the abandoned pit to inspect the remains and discern if there was anything salvageable, anything with historical significance. Moisture and decay welded the posters to the concrete walls where they hung rendering them unmovable. Unfortunately, and disappointingly for the historians, there was nothing but blocks of wet concrete and broken rebar left above ground to be hauled away to the landfill. Everything in there was saturated with mold and decay - stacks of wet sand bags, soggy remains of cardboard boxes of supplies, piles of moldy cots and blankets – nothing was salvageable, except that one 36 inch piece of curved rebar that is displayed in the museum today.—

After all, the place was originally designed to hold water!

—

The photograph at the beginning of this story shows the City demolishing the Civil Defense Shelter in 2007

Thanks go to contributors to this article: Museum of History Director Donnie Barrett; Fairhope City Clerk Lisa Hanks; Police Chief Jim Pettis; City Inspector Tom Odom; Single Tax President Larry Thomas; Retired City Employee Billy Joe Godard; ; Mrs. Shirley Nolte Davenport; Retired Police Officer Mike Randall

Dot Bremer, *Published in the Friends of the Fairhope Museum of History Newsletter, Vol. 5, Issue 3, June 2013*

Chapter 33

Barney Gaston – Fairhope's WWII Hero

The grave marker of 2nd Lt. Ernest Berry "Barney" Gaston II stands in the Southwest corner of the Fairhope cemetery and is the spot where Museum Director Donnie Barrett ends his cemetery tours talking about the Gastons and Fairhope's WWII hero. Barney was killed in the crash of his P-47 fighter airplane while attacking a German armored column approaching the town of Sivry, France. He destroyed the lead German vehicles which stopped the Germans in their tracks and they retreated. Barney's plane was apparently hit by German fire then clipped a tree top and crashed nearby in view of most of the residents of Sivry. As Germans retreated, the people rushed out to the crash site to help the pilot who had surely saved their village and their lives. Barney had been thrown clear of the plane but was dead. The first to reach him was a young girl who placed flowers on his body. Each year during the last weekend of August the people of Sivry celebrate their liberation from the Germans including a parade with flower bouquets honoring the American flier. They later erected a monument to Barney.

Mr. Barrett goes on to detail that the mayor of Sivry wrote to the mayor of Fairhope describing Barney's heroism and how his attack saved Sivry from sure destruction. The Mayor invited the Gastons and all other residents of Fairhope to visit Sivry and see the battlefield where Barney died.   Several accepted and brought home pieces of wreckage and other items. Barney's body was returned to Fairhope in 1948 and buried with full military honors. Many of the Gaston family's keepsakes were on display in the WWII exhibit at the Fairhope Museum in 2013.

The story of how Barney went from an 18-year-old high school graduate to a daring and courageous fighter pilot a year later, shows what an exceptional young man he was. Some recall that he was a member of the Fairhope elite, being the son of Spider Gaston and the grandson of founder E. B. Gaston, for whom he was named. "Prince-royal" was what he was often called. Barney was smart, talented, easy going, and well liked by everyone.

WWII started in December 1941, during Barney's senior year, but he stayed in school to graduate and then joined the Army Air Corp in the summer of 1942 with the dream of becoming a fighter pilot. He passed all the tests, examinations, and interviews to become an aviation cadet and started his military and flight training within a few months. Barney finished pilot training in February, 1944, getting his wings and a 2nd Lieutenant's Commission. Being near the top of his class, he was selected to be a fighter pilot and would spend a few weeks of specialized training in the P-47 fighter/bomber aircraft before going to Europe, to be part of the newly formed 9[Th] Air Force. He arrived in time to support the D-day invasion of France.

The 9th Air Force with its thirty-nine squadrons of P-47 aircraft, was dedicated to close air support and was a critical element of Gen. Patton's 3rd Army race across France. The P-47s would fly out in front of the U.S. Army, attacking German Army units on the march and in their fortified positions. They would bomb and strafe at tree top level, close enough to see the enemy they were killing. The Germans usually shot back with very effective anti-aircraft weapons. Many airplanes were lost, but the Germans were always destroyed. The psychological strain on the P- 47 pilots was enormous as they faced death every time they went into the air.

Barney's squadron had thirty-five pilots and they kept track of them and the missions they flew on a large board. The last column on the board was an image of an hour glass which would have all the sand in the bottom when the pilot was killed or missing. Barney's time ran out on his 25th mission, the 26th of August when his squadron was attacking the German column at Sivry, France. The squadron lost forty-four pilots by the end of the war in May 1945.

Barney takes his place as a hero in America's Greatest Generation. Going from a fun loving high school graduate, to a skilled pilot, to an aggressive fighter pilot, to killed-in-action - all in a space of two years. Barney is one of Fairhope's heroes of WWII and his story is worthy to be retold on every cemetery tour.

Curt Cochran, *Published in the Friends of the Fairhope Museum of History Newsletter, Vol. Issue 5, October – November 2016*

Chapter 34

Fairhope Golf History - the Untold Story

Fairhope opened its first golf course in 1916; twenty-one years after the founding of the Single-Tax Colony. The course was built between Fairhope and Morphy Streets, as the *Fairhope, Golf, Gun and Country Club*. This was the "focal point of golf and social life in our community," said the *Fairhope Courier* on January 5, 1923. The course was closed in the late 1950s when the land was returned to the Single Tax Corporation for housing development. For thirty years, residents turned their attention to other golf courses less convenient, or to the Bay for their outdoor activities.

In 1985, there was an attempt to bring golf back to Fairhope on land "to be donated" by Angelo Corte, Fred Corte and Madeline Berglin. But in July 1985, the Fairhope City Council voted to cancel all plans to construct an 18-hole course on donated land. The City later bought land off Highway 181 and built Quail Creek, a municipal course that opened April 4, 1988.

That is the public story of Fairhope's municipal golf. But, what happened to the "to be donated" land?

Mr. A.A. Corte, began buying Rock Creek land north-northeast of downtown Fairhope, in 1876. In 1992, Olympia Corte-Dyas, the granddaughter of Mr. Corte, sold the land, part of which was the controversial "to be donated land," to Mr. David Head. Mr. Head hired Earl Stone, a well-known Southern golf course architect, to design and build a 7000-yard championship golf course as the central part of the planned Rock Creek housing development, an upscale community that would have one thousand homes by 2013. It was common practice at the time, to have as many houses as possible on the course to improve the aesthetics and increase the value of those lots and homes. The golf course wound through the neighborhoods and crossed Rock Creek four times. The four wooden golf cart bridges that cross the swampy areas of the creek bed are up to one hundred yards long, to give the course a quaint appearance. Almost all of the eighteen golf holes go uphill or downhill, which give it a challenging look and increases the difficulty. Most of the trees and other vegetation along the golf course and Rock Creek were left in their natural state to provide a habitat for the local wildlife including fish, turtles and a beaver dam. Over seeding with rye grass in the fall keeps the course green all year round.

From the beginning, the Rock Creek golf course was a semi-private, selling memberships while remaining open to the public on a fee per golf-round basis. Most of the members are year-round residents and play golf throughout the year. Faulkner State College uses Rock Creek as a home golf course for their collegiate golf team. Bubba Watson, the well known professional golfer, played at Rock Creek while he attended Faulkner and some long-time members still remember him on the course.
The Rock Creek community grew rapidly in the boom times of the 1990s. Mr. Head sold the course in 1999 to Honors Golf, a start-up golf company at the time. Unfortunately, Honors Golf got into the business just before the downturn in the housing market. The boom times for golf and the U.S. economy suffered a major setback in 2001.

A Decade of Stories

The Rock Creek golf course was also substantially affected by Hurricane *Ivan* in 2004 and *Katrina* in 2005. Consequently, the course had to close for several months for clean up and repairs. This significantly decreased the number of people playing golf. While still recovering from the effects of the hurricanes, there was another setback in the economy in 2008, then the Gulf oil spill in 2010 deterred visitors from the Gulf Coast. The Rock Creek golf course is sustaining well now, and the community has maintained very high standards through the difficult times.

As for golf in Fairhope, there are now two courses available to citizens and guests - Rock Creek, *almost* destined to be a municipal course on "donated land", and Quail Creek, the Fairhope municipal course, both providing great entertainment on a sunny afternoon!

Curt Cochran & Bob Glennon, *Published in the Fairhope Museum of History Newsletter, Vol. 6, Issue 1, February – March 2015*

Chapter 35

History of Mardi Gras on Mobile Bay

Maids of Jubilee Float, 2013

Mardi Gras will be celebrated on *Shrove Tuesday*! When Gulf Coast Newspaper articles start printing Mardi Gras news and the schedule of parades for Gulf Shores and Fairhope, visitors to our area will probably think that these small towns are copying New Orleans, just trying to add a few parties in the slow winter months. The facts are quite different! Mardi Gras was first celebrated in the Gulf South when the French arrived at Mobile Bay in 1699, almost twenty years before New Orleans was a city. The parades get larger and more elaborate each year as typified by the photo of a Fairhope float in 2013. Mardi Gras in New Orleans which now overshadows all of the

Gulf Coast celebrations, began in the 1840s and was initiated by a group of business men who moved there from Mobile.

The origins of Mardi Gras can be traced to ancient times with the earliest being the Egyptian goddess Hathor, a cow deity, associated with joy and feasting. A second origin is taken from the Old Testament with the story of the Israelites and the golden calf in which Aaron said, "Tomorrow there will be a festival to the LORD." These are ancient traditions of feasting. The more modern tradition of Mardi Gras began with the Renaissance in the 1600s when the Catholic Church allowed some feasting before the fasting for Lent. The French term *Mardi Gras* translates to Fat Tuesday in English. For contemporary Christians, Shrove Tuesday is the day before Lent starts on Ash Wednesday. The name *Shrove* comes from the middle English word "shriven," meaning to go to confession to say sorry for sins. Lent always starts on Wednesday, so people go to confession the day before. This became known as Shriven Tuesday, then later, Shrove Tuesday.

The Mardi Gras season in other countries, especially South American is called "Carnival," which in Latin means goodbye to the meat. Mardi Gras was well established in Europe when it was first celebrated in the US in 1699, when Brothers, Pierre Le Moyne d'Iberville and Jean-Baptiste de Bienville, first came to the current Alabama Gulf Coast. By 1703, the Le Moyne brothers had established a settlement at 27 Mile Bluff, north of Mobile and held a Mardi Gras celebration there which was the beginning of the American Mardi Gras tradition. These early celebrations involved a fatted ox which was probably paraded as well as cooked. The 1704 Mardi Gras celebration included a masked ball *[sic]* (bull) and was called the "Boeuf Gras" (fatted ox). This Boeuf Gras celebration held the first known parade in Mobile when the city moved to its present location in 1711 with the parade going down Dauphin St. with 16 men pushing a cart carrying a large papier-mâché cow's head. The Mardi Gras celebrations continued in the French tradition for some fifty years until the British took over West Florida, including Mobile, in 1763. The outlandish French Mardi Gras celebration became the somber Shrove Tuesdays. Mardi Gras ceased to be celebrated on the

Gulf Coast until well after the entire area became part of the United States in the Nineteenth Century.

The rebirth of Mardi Gras in Mobile began in 1830 when a Mobillian named Michael Kraft and some of his friends were having an inebriated New Year's party and decided to raid a hardware store taking rakes, hoes and cow bells and paraded through Mobile to the Mayor's house. The Mayor liked the party and joined in. The Mayor decided to make it an annual affair, but had it moved to Fat Tuesday. This group of revelers organized themselves into the Cowbellion de Rakin Society, which was the first formally organized masked mystic society in the United States to celebrate with a parade. The idea of mystic societies was exported to New Orleans in 1856 when six businessmen, three who were formerly from Mobile, gathered at a club room in New Orleans's French Quarter to organize a secret society, inspired by the Cowbellion de Rakin Society. The Mardi Gras grew from this start and by 1840 the Fat Tuesday parade included floats with images of heathen gods and goddesses. These Mardi Gras celebrations continued to grow until the start of the Civil War in 1861. At the conclusion of 1861 parade, the Cowbellion de Rakin Society symbolically sacrificed their lead float, a paper-mache bull to the war effort. There were no more Mardi Gras parades or celebration until after the war was over.

The revival of Mardi Gras in Mobile after the Civil War is credited to another remarkable man, Joe Cain, who drove (paraded) a coal wagon through downtown during Mardi Gras season in 1866 to taunt the occupying Union Solders in a relatively safe way. The next year, 1867, the Order of Myths Society was established and organized a Mardi Gras parade choosing as their emblem the South's defeat in the War (Folly chasing Death around the broken pillar of life). This was quickly followed with the Infant Mystics Society in 1868 and the Royal Court with King Felix, the King of Frivolity, in 1872.

Mardi Gras continued to grow and become integrated with the other social events in Mobile. The Social season began as early as November. Much of the social elite in Mobile were planters who moved into their winter houses in Mobile after the cotton crops were sold. The winter months made for a very active social season with holiday parties, Debutante Balls, the Camilla Ball, and the many dances and celebrations associated with Mardi Gras, and has continued into the modern era although the social makeup of Mobile has changed.

The first Mardi Gras parade by a Black Society was in 1938 which has led to enormous growth of Mardi Gras organizations in the Black community. The Mobile Area Mardi Gras Association organizes all the parades and oversees the crowning of the King and his court.

In 1967, The Joe Cain parade was scheduled on the Sunday before Fat Tuesday to honor the man credited with bringing Mardi Gras back after the Civil War. The lead float traditionally, is the coal wagon and the parade leader is Chief Slacabamorinico, a fictitious Indian chief who escaped the Indian removal, which represented Southern resiliency.

Fairhope, as well as other Eastern Shore cities, joined in the seasonal celebration with parades and balls. The Fairhope Knights of Ecor Rouge Society was organized in 1985, the Maids of Jubilee in 1989 and the Order of Mystic Magnolias in 1992. All have grown into large organizations that sponsor elaborate parades during the Mardi Gras season.

There are several traditions of Mardi Gras that are part of most parades and balls:

Jesters: This is the most common costume for the parades and dates back to the 1600s when court jesters were popular figures and participated in most public events.

Masks: The masks date back to Greek plays when masks were held up to show the emotions of the actors. They became part of the European Balls to add anonymity to the revelers who were often inebriated and exhibited outrageous behavior.

Throws: Throws are a relatively recent addition to Mardi Gras parades with doubloons being the first throw in 1965. Of late, beads and moon pies are the most popular, with stuffed animals, cups, frisbees and a few other items close behind.

Colors: Gold and Purple are royal colors and were always part of Mardi Gras, with Green (from New Orleans) added as a third royal color of the Russian Monarchy.

Museum Director Barrett with the emblem of the
Knights of Ecor Rouge, Fairhope's oldest Krewe

King Cakes. Sweets were always part of the feasting, but the Mobile tradition of the King Cake, which has a small figurine baked in the cake, began in the 1950's by Mr. Polman. The person who gets the piece of cake with the figurine is supposed to hold the next Mardi Gras party.

The Mardi Gras parades and parties in the small towns around Mobile Bay are carrying on the traditions that began here in 1699 and are having a great time!

Curt Cochran, *Published in the Friends of the Fairhope Museum of History Newsletter, Volume 5, Issue 1 February – March 2014*

Chapter 36

Fairhope Architecture

Say the word, "Architecture" and your mind might go to the Flatiron building in New York, the Golden Gate Bridge in San Francisco, or Falling Water, the Frank Lloyd Wright house in Pennsylvania. But Fairhope residents don't have to go so far to see interesting architecture, for Fairhope has its own, albeit more modest.

The E.B. Gaston house at 118 Magnolia was built in 1910 and has the floor plan and steep roof typical of the 19th Century Mid-Western house style familiar to the early Fairhope settlers who came from that area. The steep roof allows the snow to slide  off in the bitter winters up there. Not really necessary in Fairhope. It is one of the oldest structures in Fairhope. Gaston built it on "the outside of town."

Brenny's Jewelry shop at 333 Fairhope Avenue was built in 1914 and exhibits a tall flat front, typical of many early business structures in downtown Fairhope around 1900. You see similar structures in early photographs from the frontier days out West, and in cowboy movies! The Roman style brick used for the façade of the shop was made locally at Clay City. The original equipment used to create these bricks can be seen in the museum.

The American Legion building at 400 South Mobile Street was built in 1912 for the Business Woman's Club of Mobile and was called "Pine Needles'. Early photographs show ladies gathered on the porch (No doubt discussing business!) and attractive woodwork decorating the building. The first and second story porches have been enclosed, but some of the early architectural details can still be seen.

The two houses on the South East corner of Fels Avenue and South Mobile Street are Sears Roebuck houses. Between 1908 and 1940 Sears Roebuck, together with other manufacturers, produced prefabricated houses. The parts, each individually labeled, together with nails, bolts, etc. were shipped to the house site to be assembled according to a plan. Different styles were available. The records of these sales were not being kept by Sears, but there are other Sears Roebuck houses in the area. Also on Fels Ave. is the First Church of Christ, Scientist, built in 1923 in the Egyptian Revival style. This style became popular following Napoleon's invasion of Egypt and continued with the discovery of King Tut's tomb in 1922.

And Fairhope has its own Frank Lloyd Wright connection! The house

at number 7 Laraway Lane was designed by a former Frank Lloyd Wright pupil and associate, who later lived in Fairhope. While modest in size, the half-bricked walls and large overhanging roof resemble a Frank Lloyd Wright house and the structure fits right in to the Fairhope scenery.

Our own museum building deserves a mention too. Built in the Spanish Mission Revival style in 1928, the architect had visited St Augustine Florida and had seen Spanish revival style there and introduced it to Fairhope. The George Dyson house at 505 Morphy is in the same style. There are other Spanish mission/Spanish colonial style houses in Fairhope.

Hidden away behind the trees on Oak Avenue is the whimsical house of Craig Sheldon. Built of local rock with a tower and a multicolored shingle roof, the house looks like it is from a child's nursery tale. To complement it, Craig's daughter Pagan and son-in-law Dean Mosher, have built a similar house across the road with a bridge for good measure. You expect to see a knight in shining armor ride across the bridge on a white charger!

The architecture of Fairhope exhibits the progressive nature of the early Fairhope settlers and their sense of adventure, which continues to this day.

Michael Titford, *Published in the Friends of the Fairhope Museum of History Newsletter, Vol. 9, Issue 1, February – March 2018*

Craig Sheldon Home

Chapter 37

The Story of Magnolia Beach Park

Magnolia Beach Cottages - 1911

The lovely Magnolia Beach Park is enjoyed by many Fairhopians as they walk the winding sidewalk or go down to the beach to play in the sand or swim. The story of how in became and remained a park shows the spirit of the early Fairhopers and their appreciation of parks.

The beach front land from Pier St to Laurel Ave belonged to the beach front cottages along what is now Mobile St. (then called Beach View Ave) and was used for bath houses and board walks to the beach. Museum Director, Donnie Barrett, always talks about the bath houses and bathing in the bay during his July bus tours of Fairhope. Early on, the cottages owners decided they should preserve the beach front as a park and split of the beach front areas and combined them into one block of land and filed a document in the Probate Records of Baldwin Co. as a land deed and dedicating it as a park. This document was dated March 25, 1911 and referred to the land as Magnolia Beach.

During the hard times of the 1930's, the Mobile St residents got behind in their taxes on the Magnolia Beach Park. A public-spirited man, Paul Frederick a city councilman, arranged for the city of Fairhope to acquire title to the property in 1934. The Fairhope Single Tax Colony had deeded their parklands to the city of Fairhope in 1932. All went well until 1962 when the Elks Lodge building burned and their leaders decided they would like to build their new facility

on the beach front next to the American Legion building and move Mobile Street behind their building. It would straighten Mobile Street.

The Elks Lodge leaders approached the city and did purchase the beach front area in front of their building. The Fairhope officials claimed that they didn't need the park and could sell it. They even passed a city ordinance to allow the sale. When other Fairhope residents learned of the deal, they protested loudly. Making no progress, they formed the "Association for the Preservation of the Parks" led by former mayor E. B. Overton to stop what was going on. The association sued the Elks Lodge and the City of Fairhope to invalidate the sale. The City's primary defense was that the city council had passed an ordinance. The lower courts agreed with the city so the Association appealed to the Alabama Supreme Court. The Supreme Court reversed the decision writing that the City had to let lands dedicated as parks remain park and declared the deed to the Elks Lodge to be null and void.

The Alabama Supreme Court decision dated 25 January 1965 was referenced in a Fairhope Courier article declaring the "City Deed to Elks Lodge Declared Unconstitutional". Mayor Overton said in an interview that there were no hard feelings although it cost the association $1000.00 to prevent something that never should have happened. The Elks lodge was rebuilt on the same location and there is still a curve on Mobile St.

Curt Cochran, *Published in the Friends of the Fairhope Museum of History Newsletter, Vol. 7, Issue 6, December 2016 – January 2017*

Chapter 38

The History of Law Enforcement in Fairhope

A civic minded group of Northerners made their way up from Battle's Wharf after unloading all of their belongings from the bayboat, *Jas A. Carney*. The settlement of the Single Tax Colony of *Fairhope* was taking root. They were mostly city folks, but some brought guns for shooting game and perhaps personal security, since the newcomers, mostly from Iowa, didn't know what to expect in this new land by the bay. From 1894 to 1904, the community spent its resources building and getting organized for the single tax experiment. They were a spirited group, but tolerant. Law enforcement was generally the Golden Rule: *Do unto others...*

The only sobering civil event that happened early on, was the drowning of John Hunnell, found floating in the bay on July 4, 1895. Residents dismantled a picnic table, made a casket and had a funeral. Otherwise, everyone tended to their own matters through the early years. There were heated debates and occasions of raucous behavior, but these were squelched by neighbors coming to take the wrangling citizens home for dinner, or to dry out on their own front porch. In 1904, the Single Tax Corporation was formed and law and order was managed by residents who helped one-another. Citizens felt that they had to solve their own problems anyway, now that the county sheriff and courthouse were all the way up in Bay Minette; a day's carriage ride away.

Everyone in Fairhope was not a Single-Taxer and the backlash vote against the community property and economic experiment folks, gained momentum and the need for conventional government was founded. In 1908, the Single Tax Corporation and the City of Fairhope found a way to coexist. The first city mayor was Major Harris Greeno, a former U.S. Army officer in the War Between the States, defeated E.B. Gaston, the leader of the Single Tax Corporation.

With city government, came municipal law enforcement. The first town sheriff was Ernest Dean Swift, who had no gun, vehicle nor shoes. The expensive horseless carriage was just being invented and it seemed a bit extravagant to build a livery stable to buy, house and feed a horse. So Mr. Swift walked or ran to respond to any call that came by shouts, gun shot in the air, alarm bell, or via Dr. Merchon's new fangled telephone system.

On July 10, 1908, the city's criminal docket shows that the first arrest was for drunkenness; it included a fine for "one of our town's gentlemen," of five dollars. Whether he was confined or not, is not stated, but the jail at the time was portable, made of wood and was moved wherever it was needed. That was, until an inebriated inmate burned it down. Signaling an emergency became easier when the city got electric service in 1915. If anyone needed action from the sheriff, they now simply blinked the lights twice and Mr. Swift came running.

William Steele became the town sheriff in 1924 and served for three years. He philosophically proclaimed that a horse was better for taking you home after drinking than an automobile. The car would end up in the ditch; no problem for the horse.

 In 1928, the first police station, firehouse, city hall and Public Works took up residence in the newly constructed city hall at 24 N. Section Street. This Spanish Mission Revival style building is now the Fairhope Museum of History. The police department was located on the ground floor of the building, past the mayor's desk, behind a metal wall. The original safe, on display at the Museum, inscribed "Town of Fairhope," was built into a closet near the Section St. entrance.

The jail, still in its original 1928 location, was used to house inmates until 2002 when the police department moved across Section Street. The original cells are believed to have been built using doors and bars from the old county jail that stood in Daphne until 1901.

Jack Titus became "Town Marshal" in the 1930s and continued until the early 1940s. The marshal lost the use of his right arm after a drunken butcher reportedly paralyzed him during an arrest. He had what was described as "a very mean monkey," in his office to "help keep the prisoners in." He also had a vicious little dog that went with him on all his calls.

In the1930s more jail cells were built in the police department near the current Museum elevator. Those cells were made of Clay City tiles. Only a few of the popular tiles remain, surrounding the two cells there today. The outer tile cells were demolished in 2007 when the building was reconfigured for museum use.

The first uniformed officer of Fairhope was Albert Funk in the early 1940s. During this time, Mayor Ruge was known to have slot machines in his *Blue Light* service station, store and sandwich shop. The Fairhope city council voted and declared, "No one cares anything about that state law" and the mayor was allowed to keep his slots. Not long thereafter however, they reportedly could be seen in Fly Creek at low tide.

More space was needed in the City Hall building. The original fire truck bay that you see today, became the city clerk's office and a cell for female inmates; a lean-to was built on the north side of the building (now a bank driveway) to house the fire truck. The outline of the women's jail (about 7' x 16') can still be seen when you look up at the ceiling behind the fire truck.

Police Chief McLaurin had four men and the first police car in 1946. The chief reported that, "Traffic is our big problem, as eight-hundred cars daily drive through our town. Major crime and juvenile delinquency are a thing of the past."

By 1957, the police department had five men. Bud Gilheart joined the force and was promoted to Chief in 1963. Jean White was one of the first female officers in the Police Department in the 1970s. By the 80s and 90s, there were several woman working for the department.

In 1974, city government moved out of the building, leaving 24 N. Section Street entirely to the police department. The police safe sat in the corner downstairs. The city clerk was the only person who knew the combination and she died suddenly, taking the combination with her.

The safe sat unopened for the next 37 years! In 2011, it was opened by a professional security firm and several tattered bags of marijuana used as court evidence, were found inside.

The police department bought its first Galvanometer breath analyzer in 1975. By 1977, the Fairhope police department had twelve men and women.

In 1978, the old city hall was renovated into a modern police facility. An institutional kitchen with stainless steel appliances was added in the back corner of the building next to the Clay City tile cell block. Inmates would wash city vehicles out back, behind the building.

In 1980, the Fairhope police department bought ten bullet proof vests and four helmets. Henry Nolte, who joined the force in 1958, became police chief in 1985. He served as chief until 1989, when Jerry Anderson

took over. He had been on the police force since 1965 and served as chief until 2002. He was the last chief to work in the building that began as city hall. On May 31, 2002, the Fairhope police department moved into its new facility at 107 North Section Street, next to city hall.

Joe Petties started working for the city in 1982. He became an officer in 1991 and was promoted to police chief in 2013. Chief Pettis, a native Fairhopean, now proudly serves as our Chief of Police. He has earned a faithful following of officers and citizens. ~

Research by Donnie Barrett, story by Bob Glennon, *Published in the Friends of the Fairhope Museum of History Newsletter, Vol 8, Issue 6, December 2017 – January 2918*

Chapter 39

Does the Old Daphne Courthouse **Jail** reside in Fairhope?

It was in 1901 that J.D. Hand, a Bay Minette entrepreneur did the sinister deed of coaxing the Alabama Legislature to move the Baldwin County Courthouse from Daphne to Bay Minette. On October 10 - 11, 1901, he and a band of men from North Baldwin came to Daphne under cover of night and the next morning, took the courthouse safe and records, disassembled the jail and took them to Bay Minette against the will of Eastern Shore residents. That's background, but for now, we are talking "**Jail**."

Since 2008, when our Fairhope Museum of History moved into the Old City Hall, there has been conjecture about where our old jail came from. The most frequent told story is that the cells came from a concrete ship that was built, or dismantled, in Mobile, after WWI. The reason in most minds is that the iron bars are bolted together in the corners, the floor and overhead appear to be steel plates, it's painted gunmetal gray and it is conspicuously old. The etching of initials and words are the authentic handiwork of the residents over the years.

Of the twelve concrete ships that were built nationwide as a part of the Emergency Fleet of WWI, only two were built in Mobile. We don't know which were built here, but all twelve are accounted for:

-   seven are now sunk and decaying on the ocean floor, *none* near Mobile (nearest is Galveston)
-   three were last seen as oil barges in Louisiana
-   one is a floating breakwater in CA.
-   one is still a 10-room floating hotel in Cuba

All concrete ships built in Mobile were commercial ships. None had jails that were removed or available to Fairhope; after all, Fairhope was only thirty-one years old when the jail bars were acquired.

We asked retired Chief Warrant Officer and Marine Inspector Jeff Penninger, of the U.S. Coast Guard-Mobile and fellow Fairhopean, to look at our jail cells to see if there are any clues of nautical heritage. "It looks like a brig alright, but there is nothing to indicate that it came from a ship," Jeff offered. So the search for history continued.

The fact that the Daphne Courthouse jail was bolted together remains our most intriguing clue. Particularly since the original design of the Old City Hall jail was documented in City records to be made of hollow tile. The Fairhope City Council Minutes dated March, 1922, show that Councilwoman Brown was tasked to "get an estimated cost of constructing a jail of hollow tile, for a jail to be 10 ft X 18 ft outside and eight ft high." The councilwoman made a report on the approximate cost of constructing a jail of hollow tile, later mentioned to be $4,000. The matter of jail construction was not mentioned in the Council records again for over 3 years.

Engineering and construction of the Fairhope City Hall and jail took place in 1925 - 28. On September 14, 1925, for no defined reason, City Council minutes showed that "the Marshal *[Titus]* reported the jail cells in Bay Minette to be in good condition and that same could be secured by applying to the County Commissioners." A motion was made by Councilman Mershon to meet with County Commissioners to discuss the matter of purchasing cells." The City made application for a steel cell and door. By now, it was possibly realized that a real villain could easily knock down the hollow tile wall and "terrorize the town."

In Bay Minette, the County Commission records of October 8, 1925, show that the City of Fairhope could have *(take possession of)* the cell(s), provided they "would not injure the building or *[incur]* cost to Baldwin County." On October 12, 1925, the Fairhope City Council made a motion "that *[Councilman]* Mershon be empowered to have someone in Bay Minette *take the cells apart.*" They were hauled to Fairhope at Fairhope expense and assembled in the new Fairhope City Hall in their current location. The number of cells or flat iron for windows or doors was not documented.

Today, you can visit *our* jail and see the "assembled" corners of the original Fairhope jail.

The historical facts are:
(1) The jail in Daphne's Courthouse was "disassembled" in 1901 and taken! This is amplified in the details of the raid by Mr. Hand. The details are documented by all journals of the time; *the Baldwin Times, The American Banner*, and the more recent, Judge Charles Partin's documentary account of the event; all recorded that the jail was "disassembled". When the men showed up under false pretenses, the Sheriff discovered their plan and locked them in the cells. Since they were now inside the cells

carrying tools, they began to disassemble the jail from the inside. Over the sheriff's objection, the men loaded the ox carts with the jail, the county safe, all records and furniture. This pillaging continued through Friday and Saturday. The wagons returned to Bay Minette and the jail was reassembled in a wooden house on Hoyle Street, adjacent to the new Courthouse under construction on two and a half acres of Hand's donated land;

(2) The price quote obtained by Councilwoman Brown for City Hall and jail was $4,000. The finished costs were $4,200. The hollow tile was not designed to withstand horizontal stress. Even with the wall, the City likely learned that it needed to reinforce the wall. Acquiring the free jail *late* in the construction process, was a cost savings idea, to reinforce the hollow wall, doable even after the wall was erected;

(3) The 1901 wooden building containing the "assembled" jail in Bay Minette, was demolished in 1911. The old iron bars of the original jail, "four cells with flat bars on the windows," were moved upstairs in that new jail built on Hand Street in 1911-1912. This is documented in the Baldwin Co Archives. The new jail was overbuilt and refurbished at that same location "several times" over the next seventy-five years, but no records can be found as to the whereabouts of the old jail bars - *except* for the Fairhope City records. Taylor "Red" Wilkins, a well-respected Bay Minette attorney, while a youngster with his dad as Sheriff in 1948, saw and played in that county jail. When shown photos of the Fairhope jail, he said, "The jail *didn't* look like that." That confirmed that the old round and flat-iron jail had been removed prior to the late - '40s. The old assembled jail bars were put into storage, destroyed, or came to Fairhope. In our research, we were sent to the old Bay Minette train station where surplus items are stored, and have talked with long time county employees, but no similar iron bars, or flat iron from the jail, remains. They have been disposed of and no records can be found, *except* those in Fairhope;

(4) Our Museum has circa 1900 sales literature showing that jails of that era, were indeed assembled, not welded. Welding wasn't a standard construction practice at the turn of the 20th Century; forge welding was done by Blacksmiths, but not common for building.

No county records remain as to what happened to the old jail bars, even though interviews and physical and historical document searches have been conducted by this writer for five years. There are no other known "assembled" jail bars known to exist in the county. Others are firmly affixed vertical bars with doors, across to mortar, brick or concrete walls everywhere - *except* Fairhope.

While it cannot be <u>un</u>proven, or documented with irrefutable fact, we have a compelling case that Fairhope possesses the original jail that was taken from the Baldwin County Courthouse in Daphne on October 11, 1901. ~

Bob Glennon, *Published in the Friends of the Fairhope Museum of History Newsletter, Vol. 8, Issue 4, August – September 2017*

Chapter 40

The Flowers of Fairhope

The beautiful flowers that line the sidewalks, decorate the street crossings, hang from posts in baskets and fill many planter boxes in Fairhope's downtown are the first things that catch the visitor's eye.

Scenery and flowers have been a part of our history since this property was wilderness, but the cultivation of this ambiance has become a part of Fairhope's appeal. Many visitors as well as residents who visit the Fairhope Museum of History often ask, "How do you do that and who was the driving force behind planting these lovely flowers?" The quick answer is retired Mayor Jim Nix.

In the early 1980s, then-Mayor Nix and his family were traveling in Europe and he became inspired by the flowers in the towns and villages. When he returned to Fairhope, he talked with the city council and with their endorsement, started the flower planting program. Differing tales have been added to Mayor Nix's story over the years about where he got his ideas. The most often repeated explanation is that he was traveling in Southern France and even more specifically, Nice, France, when the flora caught his attention. Others versions give an American slant; that it was Carmel,

California, or even a town in North Carolina, where he recognized the civic pride and inviting appeal of flowers and decided to implement a plan in Fairhope.

In a recent interview, Mayor Nix recounted how the Fairhope Beautification Program took place. He is an avid traveler and on his many trips to Europe he has always been impressed with the beautiful towns and villages. He recalled that he was traveling after Hurricane *Frederic* (Sept 12th, 1979), taking a break from the massive rebuilding effort that Fairhope was undergoing to repair storm damage. As he saw the flowers in Southern Germany and England, he recalled thinking, "Fairhope can do

Ex-Mayor Jim Nix

better that this". When he returned home, he met with the City Council, telling them that Fairhope needed to start a flower planting program and the initial step was to hire a horticulturalist. The City Council agreed.

Mayor Tim Kant

The first horticulturist, Tim Kant, was hired in 1983 and given the charter to start the beautification program. And Kant, an Auburn graduate, enthusiastically promoted the new venture. The first of nine greenhouses was complete in 1985. Then a full-time landscaping staff became a part of the city work force. That staff has grown to nine, with one person devoted full-time to watering. The watering is done every day starting at 4 AM with hand equipment and a water tank truck. The number of flowers on display has also grown as the city has gained population and visitors. Now there are 110 hanging baskets, 80 flower boxes and about 50 trash container/flower boxes, in addition to the street corner and sidewalk beds. The flowers are changed at least once every season.

Tim Kant was elected Mayor of Fairhope in 2000. As mayor, he has retained his interest and oversight of the Fairhope beautification program and has been known to call city employees at all levels to give instructions, ideas and advice about the flowers and other landscaping projects. He is totally dedicated to keeping Fairhope the idyllic community in which he has spend most of his life. After being elected mayor, Mr. Kant was succeeded as city horticulturist, by Jennifer Fidler.

The flowers are predominately downtown, but these are only part of a much larger beautification effort that began after *Frederic*. The enhancement began with tree plantings, since thousands of trees were uprooted or destroyed by the hurricane.

Fairhope first received the *Tree City USA* Award in 1984 from the U.S. Forestry Service and the national Arbor Day Foundation. It continues to win that award (as recently as 2012) for its long running effort to include trees in its beautification programs and has received International awards for landscaping. In 2002, Fairhope received the national *America in Bloom Award* for its flowers. The beautification program has expanded beyond downtown to include impressive large flowerbeds on Greeno Road / Hi 98 at the corners of Fairhope and Morphy Avenues.

We also have the Rose Garden located near the Fairhope Pier that was started with private donations and built on land partially reclaimed from the bay. The fountain was built by city employees. The roses are sprayed, cut and weeded each week during growing season and the grass is mowed 3 times a week. There are over 1000 bushes and 41 varieties of roses in the garden. The national *All-America Rose Selections* organization has recognized Fairhope twice over the years for its roses and its impressive maintenance commitment.

Retired Major Nix noted that many cities have tried to emulate Fairhope's flowers, but none have come close.

A Decade of Stories

The cliché' "Take time and smell the roses" has personified Fairhope since 1894, with people coming to enjoy the scenery of our Single Tax Colony. Since 1983, we have also had the flowers...

Curt Cochran, *Published in the Friends of the Fairhope Museum of History Newsletter, Vol. 4, Issue 4, August – September 2013*

Chapter 41

The Floral Clock

Visitors often ask about the large clock two miles north of downtown on Scenic Highway 98.

The floral clock at CR 104 and Scenic 98 is indeed a part of the city's beautification program; but it is a more recent addition to the thousands of plants and flowers of Fairhope. On Thanksgiving 2013, the Committee on Public Art of the Eastern Shore Arts Center and City of Fairhope dedicated the sixty-three feet by forty-two-foot floral clock on a manicured acre of public right-of-way, as a "Welcome to Fairhope" landmark seen when entering the city from the north. The eight-foot hands of the unique clock shadow over gorgeous colorful flowers with greenery outlining the time-piece face.

Camellias from China came to the America with the Europeans in 1797 and Azaleas native to Asia, Europe and North America were first planted on Carolina plantations in the 1830s. Petunias (perennials) and annuals were brought to the U.S. by "early" South American explorers. The climate and soil in Baldwin County are "natural" for these plants.

You now see that even our flowers come from around the world to bring beauty to the history of Fairhope.

Bob Glennon, *Published in the Friends of the Fairhope Museum of History Newsletter, Vol. 7, Issue 3, June – July 2016.*

Chapter 42

Christmas in Fairhope

Cutting and decorating a local tree was the highlight of early Christmas holidays in Fairhope. After all, most residents were busy building their homes soon after landing at Battles Wharf in November 1894. Founding families celebrated the holidays, but the first mention of community festivities did not appear in the *Fairhope Courier* until 1905, when a short article in the December 29 Issue said:

Christmas at Fairhope

Christmas was appropriately celebrated at Fairhope, the celebration beginning with a Christmas tree and very attractive Christmas program at the Christian church on Friday evening. Another excellent similar program was given by the Congregational Sunday School at the Hall on Monday, Christmas evening.

The usual bountiful Christmas frenzies were enjoyed at the Fairhope House, Curtis Restaurant and Bayside Café and by family and friendly groups at the houses of the people.

However, E.B. Gaston, Editor of the *Courier,* seized the moment as early as December 15, 1901 with:

SPECIAL HOLIDAY OFFERS -one dollar is a convenient amount to send – and wonderfully convenient for me to use. Send me $1 and the names of 2 new subscribers and I will extend your own subscription a year.

The December Issue of the *Courier* in 1902 spent its typeset flaunting the virtues of the new steamboat "Fairhope" over 'the other bay steamer' for its reduction of the passenger fare to twenty-five cents and for its 'steadiness' - much superior to its competitor." And the December 1903 *Courier* carried the first full page holiday ad to "Do your holiday trading at *Mershon Brother's Fairhope's Big Store* and touting, "No need to go to Mobile."

By 1905, businesses were promoting Fairhope as a winter resort and running ads for gifts, restaurants and "Dry Stovewood". Tourists discovered the Single Tax Colony and daily bayboats from Mobile and the People's Railroad made Christmas shopping another reason to visit Fairhope.

Citizens and businesses began taking more pride in the holiday appearance of Fairhope in the 1940s, when wooden cut-outs were hung from town power poles, topped off with pine limbs. The most popular were murals that depicted the twelve-days of Christmas, posted along Section Street.

In 1962, the Eastern Shore Art Association took on the challenge to replace the old and decaying placards with forty huge colorful posters that set the Christmas scene downtown. Art subjects ranging from traditional harp-tinkling angels to comic toys were hung on the town lamp-posts. The unveiling of the new posters occurred at the end of the annual Christmas parade. While over the next months, the decorations were well received by residents and visitors. But a few of these large plywood ornaments created a stir when they crashed down onto vehicles parked below.

Christmas as we know it today, began in the 1980's. In 1984, Joyce Stowe, owner of Stowe Jewelers suggested that the city light the small trees along main street to attract business and revenue for the city. Mayor Jim Nix said that if private funds could be raised to pay the electric costs, he would see what could be done. The mayor asked the newly recruited Tim Kant, city horticulturist, and Mr. Kant noted that winter, not summer, was the only time that it *could be* done. Subsequently, utility crews installed power plugs along Fairhope Avenue and added strings of lights.

"For that first lighting," Mayor Kant recalls with a twinkle in his eye, "Mayor Nix stood on a box and announced the beginning of the holiday season; then flipped a switch and Fairhope Avenue lit up!" Immediately after Christmas, the lights were turned off and removed, so the trees could be trimmed. As the trees grew, so did the number of lights and distance for wiring. "The crews had to do their work after businesses close at 5 p.m. and be finished by 10 a.m.," says the mayor. And the impressive lights did indeed attract visitors and business! Just about every year thereafter, more lights were added and now they extend from the Fairhope pier east to Bancroft Avenue and north-south on Section

Street from the Art Center and City Hall to Morphy Street. "Soon we will likely begin to add Bancroft Avenue, now that businesses are growing along that way," says Mayor Kant.

There has been a Christmas parade with Santa as long as old-timers can remember. Santa first arrived on a fire truck in 1981, through the efforts of the Fairhope Volunteer Fire Department (FVFD). The volunteers built a wooden sleigh for St. Nick and mounted it on a fire truck for the parades. In 1983, the first "ladder" truck operated by the FVFD was in the parade. The truck was affectionately called "The Bear", as it arrived for use on January 26, 1983 - the day Coach Bear Bryant of Alabama football fame, passed away.

"The only excitement on Christmas Day in Fairhope," says Mayor Kant "was in 1986." That morning, the town was turned asunder by a cold snap that froze the water in the bay and crippled city plumbing. "City employees were called-in to repair broken pipes and assist citizens who were not able to take baths due to frozen pipes. By mid-afternoon however, we had it under control; but it was a mess for about a week as temperatures stayed in single digits."

Although the annual Arts and Craft Show is not a Christmas event, local merchants again asked the city in 1989 to leave the lights "On" from the Christmas parade, on the first Friday of December, through the Arts and Craft Show in mid-March. Mayor Kant says, "It really began when we got the clock in the '90's." Mary Tuck's husband, Lawrence had made a request that upon his death, a clock be provided to the city from his estate. This was quite a great sacrifice, as the family was not wealthy, but they loved Fairhope. So it was done with a private donation from the Tuck family." The beautiful double-face clock was set at the corner of Fairhope Avenue and Section Street. Its unveiling coincided with the lighting ceremony and the launch of the lights has continued on that first weekend in December since.

The holiday season in Fairhope is well characterized by the personalities of the town. If there was ever a "Barney Fife" in Fairhope, it was in the real-life person of Walter Heinz. Walter who lived in the Fruit and Nut District (so called for the street names). He

was recognized by everyone in the 70s and 80s for his hunched back, dribble of tobacco in the corner of his mouth and eccentricity in a lovable way. At Christmas, he would dress up in a Santa suit and walk, hunched, along main street, popping his head into shops and yelling "Ho Ho Ho", then moving on down the way. His senility caught up with him one afternoon when he drove his car from downtown to his house, running stop signs and slowing for nothing. As he pulled into his yard, a police car pulled up behind him. Walter jumped out of his car, turned to the policeman and said, "Thank goodness you are here; someone has been following me all the way home!"

And there was "Miss Frances," another eccentric and pleasant lady who always dressed in bright colors, likely with a boa around her neck, and frequently seen around town on her bicycle. Each year during the 60's and '70's, Miss Frances would unannounced, come out of no-where, appear in the middle of the annual Christmas parade, ride the entire route, then dart into an alley to disappear for hours or days, then re-appear with her free-spirited lifestyle, pulling up city flowers and planting her own in their place.

"Fairhope was just a small town," says Beth Stowe Fugard. "When somebody wanted to do something to make the town pretty, we all pitched in. It was fun!"

The original Single-Taxers have passed on, but the spirit of the Colony still sparkles during the holidays!

Bob Glennon, *Published in the Friends of the Fairhope Museum of History Newsletter, Volume 3, Issue 6, December 2012*

Chapter – 43

Jubilee!

"Jubilee! "
Photo provided by Eastern Shore Chamber of Commerce / Thigpen Photography

The excitement of Fairhope's history is never felt more than during the occurrence of a Jubilee!! Long-timers on the Eastern Shore have experienced this phenomenon all their lives; unique to only a very few locations in the world, most well known are the Eastern Shore of Alabama's Mobile Bay and the coast of Pakistan.

The call will come in the middle of the summer night - "Jubilee!!". In response, locals will pull on their closest grubby clothes and scamper, unkempt into the night air, with the largest bucket they can carry, a scoop net and lantern or flashlight. Within minutes the waters edge of Mobile Bay will be teaming with people picking up fish, crabs, shrimp, flounders and marine life that has swam or crawled ashore, seeking familiar life-sustaining salt water. The event will last from minutes to a few short hours. Then the frenzy will vanish as quickly as it came!

For the Jubilee to take place, very specific conditions in atmosphere, water, tide and wind must occur. It occurs usually in the summer, in the morning before sunrise. The previous day's weather must include an overcast or cloudy day, a gentle wind from the east and a calm and slick bay surface. An incoming tide is also necessary. A combination of all of these meteorological events must take place in precise order for the Jubilee to occur.

Marine experts say that the Jubilee is caused by an upward movement of oxygen-poor bottom water forcing bottom-type fish and crustaceans ashore. Bottom water low in oxygen results from several circumstances; pockets of salty water accumulate in the deep parts of the northern portion of Mobile Bay that become stagnated during calm conditions. The stagnation is caused by salinity stratification, with the heavier salty Gulf water being overlaid by the lighter fresh river water. This prevents movement of oxygen from the air into the bottom saline water.

Due to the lack of oxygen, the Jubilee-affected fish and shellfish can not carry out normal muscular activities, such as swimming. They move slowly and seem reluctant to swim even to escape capture. However, few fish or crustaceans die during jubilees, except for those caught by those rallied out in their pajamas or grubby clothes at the sound of the alarm. There is no way of forecasting when a Jubilee will occur as only the marine life can feel the phenomenon. But when it occurs, there is little doubt that this extraordinary piece of our history is at hand!!

Jubilee in Fairhope

This photo was provided by *The Yardarm* Restaurant. *The Yardarm*, located on the town pier, is itself historic, as the buildings on the pier have accommodated bay-boat passengers since the turn of the 20th Century. Bob Pope has been owner-operator of *The Yard-arm* and Fairhope Marina for thirty-nine years. Bob says, "The marina or restaurant have had to be rebuilt after Hurricanes Frederick, Ivan and Katrina, but overall, it has been a great experience." The sunset views from the patio are reminders of why Fairhope had a "fair hope' of success" in 1894.

Bob Glennon, *Published in the Friends of the Fairhope Museum of History Newsletter, Vol. 3, Issue 5, October 2012*

Chapter 44

The Artistry of Feed Sacks
brings back memories!

Oh! Look at the beautiful color patterned dress material between the suitcases and the barrels on the rail car in the Museum! Actually, this "material" is chicken feed sacks! The people would use this cloth from the chicken feed sacks to make their clothes. I know, because our family was part of this tradition. When the chicken feed salesman would drive his truck into the farmyard, our family would all gather to see the variety of brightly colorful patterns on the feed sacks. I remember my Daddy would then say to my Mom, "What do you want me to feed the chickens this week?" She would then pick the material that she would like to use to sew some clothes. The "wise" feed salesman always made sure that he would have enough bags with the same pattern to make a complete dress. My sister Helen even won first place in her high school sewing class for the sundress (see picture) that she made from chicken feed sack

material. It was a lovely dress, but also economical - costing only fifty cents for the pattern and the thread.

Some visitors are surprised to learn of this unique use for chicken feed sacks, but others, from neighboring areas and other states, hav e stories of their own to tell. They recall their grandmothers using this chicken feed sack material to make their clothes, too. One visitor to the Museum said he had all of his shirts and shorts made from the sack material when he grew up. And he remembered that he had his first "store bought" shirt when he was a senior in high school.

Mary Ann Maradik, *Published in the Friends of the Fairhope Museum of History Newsletter, Vol 2, Issue 3, June 2011*

Chapter 45

The World of the Docent

At the very heart of the word docent is the Latin word *docere*, meaning "to teach." This is appropriate because a docent's job is to lead guests through the Museum and teach them about the history of Fairhope. So far, my experience as a docent has been more about learning than teaching. I have only been a docent at the Fairhope Museum of History for a few months, but I have already learned so much about hospitality and what it takes to run a museum. I would love to one day graduate with a master's in museum studies. I am very thankful for all of the lessons I have already learned as a student volunteer.

Ms. Peterson is a Fairhope High School Junior serving as a docent at our Museum and is interested in Museum Studies as a career.

As a docent, the number one priority is to make sure that the guests are learning and having an enjoyable time. Greeting guests and interacting with the kids that visit, are the biggest parts of being a docent. I have helped some kids unlock the safe by doing the scavenger hunt. We also offer a chance for kids to try to escape from the old jail cell. It is equally fun for them and for me to do the interactive bits on the tours. I have benefited from exercising my hospitality and communication skills, which are vital for anyone wishing to work in a museum. The guests always leave with a smile;

thanks to the wonderful docents we have at the Fairhope Museum of History.

Since I have been volunteering at the Museum, I have also done some curatorial work. Because I have an interest in working in museums in the future, Mr. Barrett has allowed me to help restore some artifacts. For example, I repaired a broken piece of pottery. I have also been lucky enough to help out a little bit with archiving some of the museum's treasures. I have archived a railroad spike and a shovel. At the previous museum where I volunteered last summer, I was never exposed to this side of the museum world. The archival process is fascinating to me and I hope that I will be able to do more work like this later on.

Another fun part of being a docent is helping with museum events. When Santa Claus flew down from the North Pole in early December to visit our Museum, I played the part of Santa's elf. Handing out candy canes and visiting with the children and families was such a fun role.

Some of the docents volunteered to participate in the Round Up Day play last November. As an attendee of the performance, I can account for the fantastic acting and the brilliant script - the work of the docents and the Museum director respectively. Event planning is a bigger part of running a museum than one would think. I learned more about the administrative side of event planning than I had anticipated. The docents are an integral part of making certain that the events are a success.

Because I have been given the opportunity to be a docent at the Fairhope Museum of History, I will be much better prepared to decide what to study in college and in which area to specialize. Being a docent is just as much about learning about museums as it is about teaching guests about the beautiful history of Fairhope.

Audrey Peterson, *Published in the Friends of the Fairhope Museum of History Newsletter, Vol. 6, Issue 1, February – March 2016*

Chapter 46

The Importance of Museums

As a child, I cherished every opportunity I had to visit museums. Museums have so much to offer in terms of content that you could spend hours or even days exploring everything. They offer a unique experience. You are able to explore the exhibits to learn; unlike reading or hearing a lecture. Museums are an important part of education because they can spark an interest or an idea in a visitor. They contribute to the community in a unique way, both academically and in terms of public education. Knowledge and awareness are so important and museums help us to achieve these. I have a deep appreciation for museums.

Fairhope is lucky to have such a great museum. Because I am planning to major in museum studies in graduate school, I have done volunteer work at two different museums. During my short time as a docent at the Fairhope Museum of History, my love for museums has only grown.

I am very excited to continue to work with the Fairhope Museum of History.

Audrey Peterson is a Fairhope High School Junior and is interested in Museum Management as a career. Director Donnie Barrett takes the initiative annually to invite students to participate in our program, to gain hands-on experience at a real progressive and fun Museum.

Audrey Peterson, *Published in the Friends of the Fairhope Museum of History Newsletter, Vol. 5, Issue 6*

Oscar
The Museum Mascot

Oscar has attended most of the museum special events, monthly meetings and one-on-one sessions, when Mary Ann Maradik, Chairperson of Docent Scheduling, and Director Donnie Barrett get together to discuss docent matters. Mary Ann is also "mom" to Oscar. Donnie Barrett dubbed him "Mascot" for his ever-presence and friendly disposition, since 2010. While he's not a relic, he is a part of the story of the Fairhope Museum of History!

Acknowledgements

This book is a composite effort of *Friends of the Fairhope Museum of History*. We appreciate the contribution made by the writers and researchers of these articles and over seventy *Friends* for their volunteer service and orchestration of the many events that have been successfully implemented through the decade of our Museum at 24 N. Section Street in Fairhope.

As Donnie often said, "We couldn't have done it without you!"

Contributing Writers

Donnie Barrett   Louie Blaze
Dot Bremer   Curt Cochran
Bob Glennon   Mary Ann Maradik
Susan Pearce   Audrey Peterson
Ralph Thayer   Michael Titford

Special thanks to Catherine King, Rita Glennon and Susan Pearce for editing these stories over the years, and to John O'Melveny Woods for applying his skill to the final formatting and preparation of this book for publication.

We also acknowledge the encouragement, imagination and fun-personality of Director Donnie Barrett. He has been a classic player-coach. He has also been a great supporter of this writer and editor, to give me free rein and editorial license to create all of our newsletters in a professional manner. He made the task a pleasure!

Robert M. Glennon

Made in the USA
Columbia, SC
12 August 2024